Arno

Help! manager

Tafelberg

© 2003 Dr Arnold Mol
Pretoria
All rights reserved. No part of this book may be
reproduced or transmitted in any form or
by any means, electronic or mechanical, including
photo-copying, recording or by any information
storage or retrieval system, without permission in writing
from the publisher
Cover illustration by Tony Grogan
Set in 10.5 on 13 pt Plantin
(Monotype Lasercomp)
Printed and bound by
Paarl Print, Oosterland Street, Paarl, South Africa
First edition 1990
Eleventh impression 2003

ISBN 0 624 02900 X

Dedicated to all the managers who have
so successfully put these theories into practice.
Without their courage
to experiment with them, these principles
would have remained mere theories

CONTENTS

Foreword

Part 1 – Introduction
1 The problem of people   3

Part 2 – Management theories
2 What do you really believe?   11
3 The three basic theories of management   15
4 The most effective theory   21
5 What is your theory?   28

Part 3 – Motivating subordinates
6 The essence of motivation   39
7 Preventing job dissatisfaction   44
8 Creating job satisfaction   52
9 A sense of achievement   63
10 Responsibility for decision making   75
11 Recognition of achievement   88

Part 4 – Managing people
12 The task of the manager   99
13 Setting objectives   107
14 Participation and delegation   121
15 Management controls   144
16 Dealing with a non-performer   154
17 Rewards that motivate   166

Part 5 – Conclusion
18 Managers make all the difference   179

Appendix   183
Bibliography   188

FOREWORD

It is fortuitous that Dr Arnold Mol's book should appear so soon after the publication of the President's Council's report on productivity in South Africa. This report stresses that productivity improvement should be accepted as the most important single long-term objective to be achieved in South Africa.

Dr Mol's book is concerned with one major aspect of productivity, namely people. In South Africa most industries are labour-intensive and consequently increasing labour productivity will make a major contribution to our economic growth. "Managing people" is a vital aspect of the management task.

From ASSOCOM's point of view we welcome this contribution because ASSOCOM has been in the forefront of encouraging the use of all our human resources without discrimination. With growing urbanisation, the scrapping of influx control and removal of the colour bar, opportunities for all are opening up. It is obviously important to develop our human resources by treating people as people, training and motivating them, rather than regarding them merely as a socio-economic factor.

This book comes at a time when our country is experiencing a critical shortage of management skills. Optimal economic development can only be achieved with sufficient manpower commanding the necessary technical know-how, skills and management abilities.

Managers in the South African context carry a heavy burden of responsibility for decisions and actions which, if rightly taken, can lead to economic growth and job opportunities. This book helps to lighten the burden of that responsibility.

Raymond Parsons
Chief Executive
ASSOCOM

Part 1
Introduction

1 THE PROBLEM OF PEOPLE

Trained for what?

When we look at the educational background of managers in South Africa today we find that the majority of them have been trained in a technical field; and I use the word "technical" in a very broad sense. The chief executives of manufacturing companies are often trained engineers. School principals are trained teachers. Medical superintendents are trained doctors. The list is endless. Yet when we talk to them about the nature of their problems, it is usually people who cause them the biggest headaches.

> One man said to me that his job as manager would be absolutely great if it weren't for his subordinates.

Time and again we find that when things go wrong in an organisation or a department it is because the person at the top is not skilled in dealing with the people working there. This holds for business enterprises as much as for organisations like schools, hospitals, churches and even sports clubs.

The reason for this is not very difficult to find. Promotion to a management position in most organisations goes to the person with the most technical expertise. The best artisan is sooner or later promoted to foreman, the best salesman becomes the sales manager, the best accountant is chosen as the next financial director, and so on. Yet technical expertise is no guarantee that the individual concerned is equipped to manage his* subordinates successfully. It is not uncommon to hear that a particular manager "is brilliant, but doesn't know how to inspire his staff".

It is a sad reflection that our educational institutions give so little attention to the whole question of managing people. It is often assumed that,

---

* The words "he" and "his" have been used throughout for ease of reading. This in no way implies that women are not suited to management roles.

once a person is trained in a particular field, he will know how to handle the necessary leadership. This point of view may stem from the perception that leadership is "simply telling subordinates what to do" – but anyone who has ever filled a managerial position will know that leadership involves a great deal more than merely "giving instructions".

The purpose of this book is to provide managers in all kinds of organisations with some practical guidelines on how to manage subordinates effectively, and particularly on how to motivate them towards a higher level of productivity.

It must be stressed that the management task is much more than "managing people". A manager has to manage materials, machinery, markets and money as well. This book therefore deals only with one aspect of a manager's task – but a vital aspect, especially in the service industry.

The problem of productivity

Compared with other developing countries South Africa's level of productivity is rather dismal. Our economic growth since 1972 is even lower than the growth rate of some of the African countries to the north. Business leaders in South Africa are constantly appealing to industry and commerce alike to raise their levels of productivity. Economists keep stressing the fact that increased productivity is the only way to bring down the inflation rate. It would not be an overexaggeration to say that increased productivity is South Africa's most important economic priority.

An increase in productivity can be achieved in several ways: better utilisation of capital and, of course, technological innovation. Most industries in our country are, however, still fairly labour-intensive – and increasing the labour productivity will not only make a major contribution to economic growth, but also lead to greater profitability. Motivating subordinates to higher levels of performance is therefore an absolute must for all managers. This is what this book is all about.

What managers would like

Most managers are very clear on what they don't want and what they do want from their subordinates:

☐ "I don't want to have to supervise my workers every day of my life."

- ☐ "I don't want to have to explain every little task to them."
- ☐ "I don't want to have to check up on everything that they do."
- ☐ "I don't want to have to rebuke them continually."
- ☐ "I want to let them get on with the job on their own."
- ☐ "I want them to be reliable and use their own initiative."
- ☐ "I want them to think for themselves."
- ☐ "I want them to accept full responsibility for their work."

These are not unrealistic expectations. Every manager would like to have these things from his subordinates, yet so few seem to get them. In fact, many managers in South Africa are very sceptical when it comes to motivating subordinates, particularly the unskilled workers. Time and again I am told by managers that I don't know what I'm talking about when I say that most workers can be motivated to far higher levels of performance. Some tell me that black workers can't be motivated because of their culture. Others tell me that female staff can't be motivated because they are interested only in their families. Some blame the unions for the negative attitude of their employees. Others, particularly in government departments, tell me that their staff cannot be motivated because of the poor pay.

Are these valid arguments? I believe not. In the past ten years I have seen tremendous increases in labour productivity in all kinds of industries, and in all parts of our country.

> In the mail-order section of a nursery in the Western Cape, unskilled workers were hired twice a year for three to four months at a time, to make up the orders that came in by mail. Each worker processed about fifty orders a day with an average of about twenty mistakes per worker.
>
> When a new supervisor was appointed she applied some of the principles set out in this book. Within three months the productivity had increased to three hundred orders a day with an average of twelve mistakes per worker.
>
> It was only then that she decided to increase the wages. Up to that point, money had not even been mentioned.

Is this an exceptional case? No, the exceptions are the cases where the right management principles have been applied and there has not been a significant improvement in performance. There are success stories and failures, but I have found that managers who claim that my principles don't work are those who have never implemented them, or they have not implemented them correctly. (I will recount some of the failures later on.)

When some articles of mine on the topic of motivating farm workers appeared in a magazine, a farmer near Pretoria went to the trouble of writing to the magazine, reporting that he had tried my principles but that they had not worked.

When I contacted him to find out why they had not worked, I discovered to my amazement (and anger) that he had not implemented a single suggestion. He would not even allow a farm worker to tie up a bunch of carrots for the market, since he would be "incapable of doing it properly".

No wonder my principles "hadn't worked".

What determines a worker's attitude?

Why are some subordinates hard-working and trustworthy, while others are lazy and unreliable? Is it the personality of the person concerned (or perhaps the way he has been brought up), or is this determined by the way he is managed?

If we say that it is mainly the personality of the individual, it would mean that a manager can do very little about the work attitudes of his subordinates. If he is fortunate enough to have the "right" kind of subordinates, he will have a motivated work force. If not, he will have to get rid of them and appoint others who do have the "right personality". In that case he will probably have to use some sort of selection test that will indicate whether an applicant has the right personality or not. And there are managers who make use of such "tests".

One manager told me that he always looks at the soles of the applicants' shoes, since he has "never met a good manager who wears rubber-soled shoes". Of course, the first thing I did when he told me that was to look at the soles of my shoes.

Another manager gives applicants for unskilled jobs his four-year-old son's jigsaw puzzle and asks them to complete the picture.

> Those who put a piece in the right place but take it out again are unsuitable because "they have no confidence". Those who try to force the pieces in, whether they fit or not, are also turned down because "they are chancers".

There are numerous selection tests available that are more scientific, but that is not the issue. I hope to show, not only from theory, but particularly from practice that a worker's attitude towards his job is determined mainly by the way he is managed, and that 90 per cent of all employees can be highly motivated.

> Please note that I did say 90 per cent of all workers. I would be naive if I claimed that all subordinates could be motivated. I estimate that there must be approximately 10 per cent of people (of all races) who will not respond positively, no matter what we do. But that is a small minority. There is enough evidence to indicate that the majority of workers can be motivated.
> A more debatable question is whether the majority of managers can be motivated to motivate their staff.

The attitude of an employee towards his work is determined by two basic factors:
- ☐ The management theory of his manager
- ☐ The design of his task

In part 2 we look at the theories managers hold, that is, the assumptions they make about their subordinates and how those beliefs influence their management styles. In part 3 we discuss the effect the actual design of the task has on the motivation of the person doing the job. Part 4 then gives a practical step-by-step description of how a manager must set about managing his subordinates.

Part 2
Management theories

2 WHAT DO YOU REALLY BELIEVE?

Every manager makes assumptions

For the purpose of this book the word "manager" is used in a very broad sense. It includes anybody who has the responsibility of supervising the work of others, regardless of whether the official job title is gang boss, matron, section head, chief typist or managing director.

One of the characteristics of managers is that, without exception, they all make assumptions about their subordinates. Every manager has certain beliefs about what his subordinates are like, what their needs are, what their motives are, etc. Furthermore, every manager has certain beliefs about how his subordinates ought to be managed. This is his "management theory".

> A foreman once told me that factory workers can only be motivated by the "five-point plan". When I asked him to elaborate, he held his fist up in a threatening manner, to indicate that they should be thrashed.
> That was his management theory!

Questionnaire on management beliefs

You may find it useful to formulate your own beliefs by completing the following questionnaire. I suggest that you write your answers down on a separate sheet of paper. Then you can ask some of your colleagues to answer the questionnaire without influencing them with your answers.

Ten groups of three statements each (A, B and C) are given. Read the three statements in each group and then allocate ten points to indicate your opinion about the relative applicability of each statement to your work situation. There are no right or wrong answers. All that matters is your point of view on your subordinates as they are at present.

Example

☐ If, for example, you strongly agree with statement B, and only slightly with statements A and C, you could perhaps allocate 8 points to statement B and 1 point each to statements A and C. You could even allocate 10 points to statement B and no points to statements A and C.

☐ If, on the other hand, the statements in a particular group seem to be equally applicable as far as your subordinates are concerned (with A perhaps slightly more relevant), you could allocate 4 points to A and 3 points to B and C, as long as the total number of points for each group adds up to 10.

Answer the questionnaire with your own work situation in mind. Although there will always be exceptions, think of how most of your subordinates are at present – and not how you would like them to be. In the same way, think in terms of the typical way in which you manage your staff at present, and not how you would like to manage. Don't spend too much time thinking through your answers. Usually the initial response is the most accurate one.

Group 1 Most of my subordinates . . .
A ___ would prefer not to be burdened with more responsibility
B ___ are keen to use their own initiative to solve work problems
C ___ get real job satisfaction when working conditions like pay, fringe benefits, equipment, etc. are favourable

Group 2 As a manager . . .
A ___ I usually have to supervise my subordinates closely
B ___ I frequently have to tell my subordinates how important they are
C ___ I always consult my subordinates on the decisions that affect their work

Group 3 Most of my subordinates . . .
A ___ want to be held responsible for their own work results
B ___ do not like hard work and will avoid it if they can
C ___ are happy in their work as long as they are treated fairly

Group 4 As a manager . . .
A ___ I usually have to take my subordinates' feelings into account when allocating work activities to them

B ___ I constantly give my subordinates as much responsibility as possible
C ___ I often have to ensure that the work procedures are carried out correctly

Group 5 Most of my subordinates . . .
A ___ are keen to show what they are capable of doing
B ___ will do their utmost when they are treated like human beings
C ___ do not have the ability to solve their own work problems

Group 6 As a manager . . .
A ___ I always have to strive to create a happy working climate for my staff
B ___ I often have to solve work problems for my subordinates
C ___ I constantly seek to utilise the talents of my subordinates to the full

Group 7 Most of my subordinates . . .
A ___ will work harder when they know that they are all treated on an equal basis
B ___ have greater intellectual abilities than their jobs actually require
C ___ would prefer someone else to shoulder the responsibility for decision making

Group 8 As a manager . . .
A ___ I frequently allow my subordinates to control the quality of their work themselves
B ___ I often have to give my subordinates detailed instructions on how to carry out their tasks
C ___ I regularly have to tell my subordinates about future plans that will affect them

Group 9 Most of my subordinates . . .
A ___ are more interested in what they earn than in what they do
B ___ want to feel that they are important to the organisation
C ___ are keen to broaden their knowledge and learn new skills

Group 10 As a manager . . .
A ___ I frequently allow my subordinates to draw up their own work plans

B _____ I usually have to be very sensitive to the personal needs of my staff
C _____ I often have to check the work of my subordinates in detail; otherwise they will make too many mistakes

(The calculation of the score will be explained later.)

3 THE THREE BASIC THEORIES OF MANAGEMENT

What managers believe

In chapter 1 I mentioned that the attitude of a worker is influenced by two factors, the first being his manager's "management theory". Every manager follows a certain management theory, whether he is conscious of it or not. This does not mean that he has studied a number of academic books and then picked a particular management style, but that every manager holds a certain set of beliefs about what his subordinates are like and how they should be managed.

These beliefs obviously differ from manager to manager, but if we could somehow collect all the assumptions that managers in South Africa hold about the people who work for them and analyse these beliefs, we would find that there are basically only three management theories. These are:
- The traditional theory
- The human relations theory
- The human resource theory

The traditional theory

This set of assumptions is known as the traditional theory because it seems to contain the most widely-held beliefs in the history of management. Managers who subscribe to this theory, for example, believe the following:
- Work is unpleasant for most of their subordinates.
  - *Workers are basically lazy and will avoid work whenever they can.*
- Most of their subordinates are interested only in money, or in what they can get out of the employer.
  - *Workers will not do anything extra without some kind of additional remuneration or benefit.*
- Most of their subordinates would prefer not to be given any responsibility for decision making.

- *Workers would rather let the manager solve the problems, or let someone else take the blame when things go wrong.*

☐ Most of their subordinates are not capable of solving their own work problems.
- *Workers are not able to think for themselves because of their lack of education/training/experience.*

It is important to understand that these beliefs are not necessarily wrong. A specific manager's subordinates may well fit these descriptions. However, what is more important is the effect that these beliefs have on a manager's behaviour towards his subordinates.

☐ If he believes that most of his subordinates are lazy, he is likely to supervise them closely.
- *"If I don't sit on their tails all day long, they won't get anything done."*

☐ If he believes that most of his subordinates are interested only in money, he will devise all kinds of incentive schemes in an effort to get more work out of them.
- *A typical example is the commission paid to salesmen. The assumption is that the opportunity to earn more will spur them on to sell more.*

☐ If he believes that most of his subordinates do not want responsibility, he will see himself as being responsible for the *thinking* and his subordinates as responsible for the *doing*.
- *I once overheard a manager say to one of his workers: "I don't want your head, I only want your hands." Such a manager obviously believes that he is there to do the thinking – they must simply do as he tells them.*

☐ If he believes that most of his subordinates are not capable of thinking for themselves, he will very likely explain each task in detail, and leave them with the instruction that they must call him as soon as any problem arises.
- *He will be reluctant to explain two steps at the same time in case they forget the first step. Such a manager also tends to reduce tasks to very simple elements on the assumption that this will reduce the likelihood of mistakes.*

I once heard of a worker who had tried to solve a problem on his own, but made a mess of it.

When his manager scolded him, the worker defended himself by saying: "But I thought . . . ", upon which the boss snapped: "You mustn't think – you must do as I tell you."

That is a manager who believes in the traditional theory.

I'm not saying that it is wrong to manage in the traditional way. It may well be necessary to do so. At this stage I am merely pointing out that the beliefs of a manager determine his behaviour. The two cannot be separated. "Faith and works go hand in hand."

The human relations theory

A set of assumptions known as the human relations theory is based on the belief that workers will be motivated when they are *treated* well – like human beings. Managers who hold this theory believe the following:
- Most of their subordinates will do their best when they are treated fairly and decently.
  – *They want to be treated like human beings.*
- Most of their subordinates want to feel that they are important to the organisation.
  – *Workers are not just replaceable "production factors" – they are individuals who want to be noticed.*
- Most of their subordinates will get job satisfaction when the working conditions are pleasant.
  – *The social needs of workers are just as important as their financial needs.*
- Most of their subordinates want to be kept informed of future events that will affect them.
  – *Workers want to know what to expect in the weeks or months that lie ahead, rather than to be told about a new task or project out of the blue.*

Again, these beliefs may be perfectly correct for a particular manager, but how will these beliefs affect his management approach?
- If he believes that his subordinates will perform well if they are treated humanely, he is likely to treat them with respect, fairness and consideration.
  – *He will, for example, have an "open door" policy, take the trouble to get to know his staff members personally, familiarise himself with various cultural differences, etc.*
- If he believes that most of his subordinates want to feel important, he will tell them regularly how important they are, or how important their work is for the organisation.
  – *He may not actually consider them to be important, but as long as he tells them, at least it will make them feel important.*
- If he believes that their social needs are just as important as their finan-

cial needs, he will encourage social activities and try to motivate his subordinates by being kind to them.
— *Typical examples are the recreational facilities that some of the larger organisations provide for their staff, or the regular social outings, office parties, etc. that are so prevalent today.*

I worked for a large organisation that believed in this theory. At their head office they provided a large range of facilities for their staff: tennis courts, swimming pool, bowling green, squash courts, table-tennis tables, badminton courts, snooker tables, hockey field, rugby field, cricket field, soccer field, and even a six-hole golf course. Later they added a ten-pin bowling alley.

In this company the management believes that "people who play together will work together" – a typical human relations theory approach.

☐ If he believes that most of his subordinates want to be kept informed, he will tell them regularly about any plans that will affect them.
— *"Next week we're going to overhaul that machine from top to bottom." "Next month we're switching over to our new computer system." "Next year we're taking two of our products off the market."*

It is obvious that the beliefs of the manager determine his management approach, but for many managers these beliefs are subconscious. They have not really sat down and analysed what it is that they really believe about their subordinates; yet those beliefs play a dominant role in their management behaviour.

Some managers will immediately identify with the human relations theory as being a "better" approach than the traditional theory. But whether the human relations theory is more effective than the traditional theory remains to be seen.

Many managers seem to consider the traditional theory and the human relations theory to be the only options available to them. Either they have to be strict and "run a tight ship" or they focus on good interpersonal relations in the hope that if they are good to their staff, they will get a positive response in the form of commitment and hard work. In South Africa many managers tend to apply the human relations theory with their white staff, but revert to the traditional theory when it comes to their black staff.

The human resource theory

There is, however, a third theory known as the human resource theory. The focus of this theory is not on treating employees well, but on *utilising* them well. Managers who hold to this theory believe the following:
- Most of their subordinates find work enjoyable if they pursue meaningful objectives.
  - *Workers actually like to work hard when they can see that they are achieving something worthwhile.*
- Most of their subordinates are keen to show what they are capable of doing.
  - *Workers like to be left alone so they can prove to the boss how good they are.*
- Most of their subordinates are more intelligent than their work requires them to be.
  - *The thinking ability of workers can be utilised to a far greater extent.*
- Most of their subordinates will be highly committed to their work when they are entrusted with responsibility.
  - *Workers will draw up their own work plans and check them afterwards to ensure that the work is done correctly.*

When some managers read these assumptions they react with scepticism and incredulity. "A bloke who believes that has obviously never worked in our type of industry." That may be true, but again we need to ask ourselves how a human resource manager views his management task.
- If he believes that his subordinates find work enjoyable when they pursue meaningful objectives, he will see it as his task to help them formulate such objectives for themselves.
  - *He will agree with them on the goals that they are going to strive for in their work.*
- If he believes that his subordinates are keen to show what they are capable of doing, he will give them the opportunity to prove themselves.
  - *He will encourage them to use their own initiative and allow them to get on with the job on their own.*
- If he believes that his subordinates are more intelligent than their work normally requires of them, he will involve them in decision making that will affect their work performance.
  - *He will encourage them to think for themselves and solve their own work problems.*
- If he believes that his subordinates will be committed to their task when they are given responsibility, he will give them that responsibility.

— *He will allow them to make their own decisions regarding plans, problems and priorities.*

Some managers respond to the human resource theory with a wistful look. "That's how it should be, but my staff aren't ready for this approach yet." While that may be a perfectly legitimate argument, I'm simply pointing out that the *beliefs* of a manager (and all managers have such beliefs) will determine his management style. The question is: "Which theory is the most effective in obtaining high levels of productivity from our subordinates?"

4 THE MOST EFFECTIVE THEORY

The most common theory

Which theory is used most frequently in South African companies? I have put this question to hundreds of managers in a large number of organisations. The answers are not always the same, but the majority seem to agree that the traditional theory is applied most often at the lower levels of the organisation (with a noticeable move towards the human relations theory in the last decade or so), while the human resource theory is usually applied at higher levels of management.

> The middle managers of a large manufacturing concern with a history of strong autocratic leadership from the top told me that in their company the traditional theory was applied at the top levels and the human resource theory at the lower levels.
> I think they are right – but this is a rare exception.

Some research was done to determine what theory most managers in the United States believe in (Miles 1975:45). The researchers found that many managers considered their subordinates "not yet ready to take decisions on their own", and they tended to rate their subordinates well below themselves on important traits like responsibility, judgment and initiative. However, when it came to rating themselves in comparison with their own superiors, many of them assessed themselves as equal to or higher than their bosses. Many expressed the opinion that their superiors were underutilising the abilities of their subordinates.

The conclusion drawn from this research was that most managers tended to hold two theories – one for themselves (the human resource theory) and another one for their subordinates (either the human relations theory or the traditional theory). Isn't it interesting that we all tend to attribute the positive qualities to ourselves, but the negative qualities to other people?

> At one management seminar in the Natal Midlands I had just introduced myself to the group when one person asked me if I had ever worked with the blacks in the Midlands. When I replied in the negative he immediately told me: "It won't work with them."
> This was before I even had a chance to tell the group what was supposed to work.

The most effective theory

More important than knowing what theories are used most often is knowing what theory will produce the best work results. I am amazed at how many managers tell me that they are convinced the human resource theory will produce the best results. What they cannot tell me is why they so seldom practise it.

Is the human resource theory the most effective one, or should we first start with the human relations theory and then gradually move on to the human resource theory? Isn't the traditional theory the best approach with certain categories of workers? Surely the "correct theory" depends on the nature of the subordinates concerned?

Absolutely correct! The theory that will produce the best work results is the theory whose assumptions are the closest to reality.

> If in reality employees are lazy, only interested in money, and unable to think for themselves, the most effective approach will undoubtedly be the traditional theory.
> If, however, employees find their work enjoyable, are keen to prove themselves, and are quite intelligent, the most effective approach will be the human resource theory.

The logical question to ask then is: "What is reality?" What are our subordinates really like? The answer is simple: "We don't know!"

This statement may be challenged by many managers but it is nevertheless true because of the phenomenon of the *self-fulfilling prophecy* in human behaviour. A prophecy is a prediction that something is going to happen in the future. A self-fulfilling prophecy is a prediction that is actually brought about by the fact that it is made.

> I can predict that the gold price will go up by at least $100 in the next twelve months. That is a prophecy, but it is not self-fulfilling. The fact that I make that prediction will not have the slightest effect on the actual price.
>
> On the other hand, a lady from a rural town may be on her way to a large city to do some Christmas shopping. En route she keeps telling herself that she is going to have an accident because of the heavy traffic. What is the likelihood of her having an accident? Very good.
>
> That is a self-fulfilling prophecy!

In the work situation if a manager believes that his subordinates are lazy, he is likely to supervise them closely. However, what do workers who are always supervised closely do when the supervisor turns his back? They sit down – or at least reduce their work performance to the absolute minimum. What does that *prove* to the supervisor? That he was right all along. They are lazy.

> A friend of mine who farms in the Eastern Transvaal saw his neighbour (who is very much a traditional manager) supervising his farm workers by watching them while they worked. My friend stopped at the side of the road to discuss something with his neighbour, and as the employer walked away, saw that all the workers stopped working.
>
> However, every now and then their boss would turn in his tracks and, as he started turning around, the workers would get into motion. The moment he resumed walking, they stopped work again.
>
> That manager had no doubts whatsoever about his subordinates' characteristics.

The self-fulfilling prophecy

If a manager believes that his subordinates are not able to think for themselves, he will not allow them to take any decisions on their own. But what do people do when the thinking is done for them? They switch off. Then one day when the supervisor is not there, and they are faced with having to solve a problem on their own, they cannot do it. Once again the manager gets the evidence that his workers are "stupid".

> The self-fulfilling prophecy applies to all kinds of people in all kinds of situations. Just see what happens in the army. Any corporal will tell you how lazy and stupid the troopies are – and he's got the "evidence" to prove it.

One of the effects of the self-fulfilling prophecy is that it can so easily limit the work capacity of workers. This is particularly true when workers are told by management how much work they are expected to perform per day or per hour. This problem is aggravated by the use of work study methods where *standard time* is estimated. This may actually limit the capacity of the job incumbents, because it tells them how much work is considered "normal". It then creates a mental block that actually prevents them from achieving more.

> In Natal the average performance of cane cutters on sugar farms is in the region of 3,5 tons a day "cut and stacked". One farmer, however, received a special productivity award from the National Productivity Institute for maintaining an average of 12 tons a day among his cane cutters.
> The reason for the difference is that the other farmers tell their cutters exactly how much they must cut on a particular day. When they reach that target, they go home. My friend allows his cutters to decide for themselves how much they will cut each day.

I am convinced that one of the major reasons for South Africa's low productivity is the fact that managers expect so little from their subordinates –

and get it. This "proves" to them that their workers are not capable of higher performance, and so the negative cycle of the self-fulfilling prophecy continues. This is particularly true when it comes to the opinion that white managers have of black workers. They cannot help managing them in accordance with what they believe. However, their management behaviour evokes a response from subordinates that "confirms" their beliefs.

> In an electronics company, applicants for factory jobs were given a finger-dexterity test as part of the selection process. There was evidence that applicants who scored high on the test turned out to be the better workers.
>
> In one experiment, however, the researchers took the names of forty new appointees. They did not look at the test scores, but picked ten names at random and put high scores next to those names. They then allocated low scores to another ten names chosen at random, and the remaining twenty names were given average scores.
>
> These "test scores" were given to the foremen to whom the newcomers were allocated. The workers themselves were not informed of their scores.
>
> Three months later the various foremen were asked to rank these new employees in terms of their productivity. Guess who was top of the list? The ten workers who had been "given" high scores on the test. What's more, the actual production figures confirmed this assessment.
>
> The only conclusion the researchers could draw was that the foremen had made an assumption based on the information they had been given. They had managed those individuals as if they were the better workers, and the workers had responded accordingly.
>
> A typical self-fulfilling prophecy!

The self-fulfilling prophecy affects every area of our lives. Doctors have known for years that a patient's rate of recovery is often determined by the patient's belief in whether he will get better or not. Numerous experiments have been done to test the effectiveness of a particular medicine, by giving one group of patients the real medicine and a second group suffering from the same disease something that they *thought* was the real medicine (e.g. coloured water with a nasty taste). In many cases both groups recovered at the same rate.

A child's performance at school is largely determined by the expectations that parents and teachers have of that child. In one classic experiment some university professors told the teachers at a primary school that children do not develop intellectually on a steady gradient, but that they develop in sudden spurts, after which they level off for a year or two, and then suddenly spurt again. They called this phenomenon "inflected acquisition", which sounded very scientific, but was in fact a lot of nonsense. Children develop on a steady upward gradient – and the professors knew this – but they told the teachers that they had developed a test which would indicate which children were about to "spurt intellectually". The test would be administered to the entire school and the teachers would be given the results.

What the teachers did not know was that the pupils were given an ordinary intelligence test. Without looking at the test results the researchers selected 20 per cent of the pupils at random and informed their respective teachers that these children were about to "spurt intellectually". The children themselves received no feedback at all.

Twelve months later the same test was administered to the entire school again, and the scores were compared with those of the first test. The major difference was in the test results of the pupils in Grade 1 and Grade 2. While the rest of the pupils in these grades had improved their scores by an average of 12,4 points, the children in the experimental group (i.e. those who had been labelled as the "spurters") had improved their scores by an average of 27,0 points. Five of them showed an increase of 40 points!

Again, the only conclusion the researchers could come to was that giving the teacher the information that a particular pupil was about to "spurt intellectually" was a self-fulfilling prophecy. The teacher started teaching the child on the assumption that he was about to develop mentally. The child sensed this and responded accordingly.

There have been numerous incidents where teachers have told specific scholars, or even entire classes, how useless they were – and the pupils respond accordingly. Such teachers usually pride themselves on the fact that they know their pupils, because they can predict quite accurately what their school performance will be like. What such teachers do not realise is that they are simply seeing the effects of a self-fulfilling prophecy.

A recommended theory

I hope to show in this book – not just theoretically, but also by means of numerous practical examples – that the human resource theory can be applied successfully to the large majority of employees at all levels in the organisation.

If that evokes scepticism it is understandable since it is rather difficult to change the opinions that managers have of their subordinates, when these opinions have been formed (and confirmed) over a period of many years. But give yourself the benefit of the doubt. If you are having trouble coping with subordinates who are not coming up to your expectations, it may be as a result of the assumptions you have made about them, and the way you have managed them.

5 WHAT IS YOUR THEORY?

It's only a questionnaire

Let's see what theory you favoured most when you answered the questionnaire in chapter 2. Before you work out your score, however, I must point out that the score should not be taken as determinative. It would be wrong to think: "The test showed that I am a human relations manager (or whatever); I must be like that." That could be just another form of the self-fulfilling prophecy.

The way you interpreted the questions, the actual subordinates you had in mind, recent incidents with individual subordinates, etc. all had an effect on your answers. Only you can decide whether your answers reflect your actual management approach or not.

Scoring your questionnaire

Write the points that you allocated to each statement on the following scoring key, and then add up the points in each of the three columns. It might be useful to write your scores on a separate sheet of paper so as not to spoil the book.

> *Note:* The sequence of the scoring key is not always A, B, C, in that order. Do not simply transfer your scores in the same sequence in which you wrote them down. Ensure that the points you allocated to A are written next to A on the scoring key, the B score next to B, etc.

Scoring key

	Traditional theory	Relations theory	Resource theory
Set 1	A ____	C ____	B ____
Set 2	A ____	B ____	C ____
Set 3	B ____	C ____	A ____
Set 4	C ____	A ____	B ____
Set 5	C ____	B ____	A ____
Set 6	B ____	A ____	C ____
Set 7	C ____	A ____	B ____
Set 8	B ____	C ____	A ____
Set 9	A ____	B ____	C ____
Set 10	C ____	B ____	A ____
Total	_____	_____	_____ = 100

What does your score mean? To arrive at a significant interpretation, you should compare your score with those of other South African managers who have also answered this questionnaire.

The traditional theory score

A score of 0-13 indicates that you are in the lower 25 per cent of the scores obtained by other managers. That means that at least 75 per cent of managers who answered this questionnaire had a score of 14 or more. If your score is lower than 13, it means that you do not put much faith in the traditional theory.

A score of 29-60 places you among the upper 25 per cent of managers. In other words, 75 per cent of managers scored lower than 29. If you scored more than 29, it means that you put a great deal more emphasis on the traditional theory than other South African managers.

A score of 14-28 places you somewhere in the middle compared with other managers. The average score for the traditional theory was 20.

The human relations theory score

A score of 0-33 places you among the lower 25 per cent of managers. That is, 75 per cent of managers who completed this questionnaire had a score of 34 or more for this particular theory. If your score was lower than 34, it means that you do not attach much importance to the human relations theory.

A score of 43-60 places you among the upper 25 per cent of managers. In other words, 75 per cent of managers had a lower score than 43. If your score was more than 42, it indicates that you have a higher regard for the human relations theory than most other South African managers.

A score of 34-42 places you somewhere in the middle in comparison with other managers. The average score for the human relations theory was 38.

The human resource theory

A score of 0-33 places you among the lower 25 per cent of managers. In other words, 75 per cent of managers who answered this questionnaire scored 34 or more on this theory. If your score was lower than 34, you do not really believe in the human resource theory.

A score of 47-60 places you in the upper 25 per cent of managers, since 75 per cent of them scored lower than 47. If your score is more than 46, it means that you put considerably more emphasis on the human resource theory than other managers in South Africa.

A score of 34-46 places you somewhere in the middle, compared with other managers. The average score for the human resource theory was 39.

One last question before I summarise these concepts: "How do you see your subordinates?" Are you there to help *them* get the work done? Or are they there to help *you* get the work done? You will have either one view or the other – you cannot have both. Please indicate with an X which view applies to you:

____ I am there to help them get the work done.
____ They are there to help me get the work done.

A comparison of the three management theories

Which two theories are most closely related to one another? Is the human relations theory closer to the human resource theory or is it closer to the traditional theory? Most managers say that the human relations theory is very closely related to the human resource theory, but they are wrong. The human relations theory is much closer to the traditional theory. Let me explain.

The *traditional manager* sees his basic management task as "making sure that the work is carried out correctly by the workers". That's it. When the tasks have been carried out satisfactorily, his management task is completed as far as he is concerned.

The traditional manager's view is that his subordinates are there to help *him* get the work done.

> When a manager holds the view that his subordinates are there to help him, who is responsible for the work? *He* is!
> Since two people cannot be responsible for the same thing, his subordinates will show very little sense of responsibility – simply because they don't have any responsibility.

The *human relations manager* also sees it as his task to ensure that his subordinates carry out their tasks in the way that is required of them. He *also* sees himself as being responsible for the work, and his subordinates as his "assistants". That's why this theory is so close to the traditional theory.

However, the human relations manager goes a step further than the traditional manager. He also sees it as his task to treat his staff well and to keep them as happy as possible in their work.

> When the subordinate of a traditional manager makes an error of judgment, he is likely to be scolded and yelled at by his boss for being such an idiot.
> When the subordinate of a human relations manager makes a costly error, his boss is very likely to say something like: "Look at all the damage you have caused. Please don't try to handle matters like this on your own in future. Call me next time and let me deal with it."

Can you see how pleasant the human relations manager was? He did not treat his subordinate in a derogatory fashion like the traditional manager. Yet in essence his approach was very similar, because the message he gave his subordinate was: "I'm here to do the *thinking*, you must just focus on the *doing*."

I am of the opinion that the human relations theory is probably the least effective approach, because it is seen by subordinates as a "soft" approach. That does not imply that employees should be treated harshly. It simply means that if a manager tries to motivate his staff *only* by treating them well, the chances are very good that they will abuse his kindness.

Another reason why the human relations approach is ineffective as a management approach is that it stems from an attitude of *paternalism*. It conveys the message to subordinates that they ought to be grateful that the "boss is so good to them". This is degrading to any person who has some measure of self-respect, and is certainly not a method to stimulate a high level of productivity.

> One of the reasons why our government leaders in the past have had very limited success in obtaining the cooperation of politicians from the other race groups stems from their paternalistic attitude towards these groups.

The *human resource manager* has a very different view of his management task. He sees it as his primary responsibility to get his subordinates to function successfully on their own. The less they need him, the more successful he has been as a manager. He obviously holds the view that he is there to help *them* get the work done – and that immediately implies that the *workers* are responsible for the work, not the manager. He is there to help them when they need him – and when they don't need him, he stays out of their way.

> After some years of using the human resource approach managers have run into the problem of not quite knowing what to do with their time, since the need for constantly checking up on their staff is no longer there.
>
> However, it isn't long before most of them get involved in management work at a higher level, which sooner or later leads to a promotion.

Another problem that the human resource manager faces is that he may occasionally forget the fact that his workers are responsible for the work. When he starts interfering with their activities, he runs the risk of being "fired" by his subordinates.

> A factory manager in Rosslyn came across some of his men trying to fix a machine that had broken down. When he started telling them how they should go about it, the foreman told him politely but firmly to go back to his office, since they were quite capable of fixing it on their own.
>
> A farmer in the Free State picked up a spanner to make some adjustments to one of his large tractors. The driver quickly took the spanner out of his hands and told him to leave the tractor alone because he was "likely to strip the threads".

Of course this would make some managers "strip *their* threads" – but these subordinates were not talking with aggression or arrogance. They were talking with *pride*, because that foreman's section had the best performance record in the factory, and that driver's tractor was running at a lower maintenance cost than it had ever run before. If you have never been "fired" by your subordinates, you have not yet achieved the ultimate success as a manager of people.

The human resource theory in practice

If the assumptions of the human resource theory seem acceptable in theory, but too good to be true in practice, I can understand the feeling of disbelief. Yet examples of its effectiveness can be found throughout South Africa.

The marketing manager of a large company in Johannesburg decided to purchase the franchise for a well-known fast-food outlet at a new shopping centre on the West Rand. He was even prepared to give up his lucrative position in order to run it, especially since he would have had to build up the business from scratch. However, he is a strong believer in the human resource theory and he decided to appoint Peter, a young black man, as the manager.

Peter, with matric certificate and all, had started his career as a storeroom cleaner, but within a few years became a salesman with a cosmetics company, where he was taught the basics of marketing. At that stage he also obtained a diploma from the Wits Business School in basic management. Naturally he jumped at the opportunity to take over the fast-food outlet.

The owner was warned by the franchising company that he was taking a very big risk, since the position was very demanding, both time-wise and management-wise. If he went ahead with his plans, Peter would be the first black manager to hold such a position in their organisation, and they were very sceptical about the chances of success. But he went ahead anyway – and so did Peter.

Initially Peter concentrated on motivating the staff to provide good customer service and to maintain a high standard of cleanliness. He regularly measured the performance of the waiters in these areas and gave them feedback on how well they were doing. The result was not only an excellent standard of service, but also a remarkably low labour turnover. But that was just the beginning. It wasn't long before Peter became involved with the food preparation, the purchasing, and eventually the entire financial administration.

Seven months after starting, Peter had achieved amazing results. His customer turnover had been increasing steadily and the books were already showing a profit.

Peter keeps a tight financial rein on his costs and the deviation of his expenses from budget averages about 3 per cent. He constantly negotiates with suppliers (37 of them in 1989) to obtain a better deal – and he has full signing powers on the cheque account.

The owner had been warned by an auditor friend that pilfering is one of the major expense items in the fast-food business. It is an accepted fact that, if a fast-food outlet is making a profit, the manager is probably taking his own cut as well – but to date the stock losses at this outlet have been minimal.

The franchising company regularly carries out a very detailed inspection of all its outlets to ensure that their own high standards are maintained. At the first inspection, Peter's outlet scored 67 per cent and he was placed eleventh out of 21 outlets in the area. Three months later he scored 79 per cent and he moved to sixth position. When Peter got the results, he just shrugged and said: "That isn't good enough!"

The shopping complex in which this operation is located has four wings with approximately fourteen stores in each wing. The merchants in Peter's wing elected him as their representative to serve as one of the four directors of the shopping centre. He is the only black director on the board.

It is important to point out that the owner did not simply hand over the business to Peter, blindly trusting him "to carry on". He keeps very stringent financial controls. That aspect can never be delegated. But what he has delegated (gradually as Peter proved his ability) is the decision-making responsibility that is required to run the business on a day-to-day basis. Whereas in the beginning he had to spend many long nights with Peter in the restaurant, he is now able to concentrate on his own job as marketing manager, and exercise sound control from a distance.

People who hear this story often say to me: "Yes, but Peter is the exception." I have to disagree; the owner is the exception. I wonder just how many "Peters" we have in our organisations – we just don't know about them or how to realise their potential.

Conclusion

The opinion that a manager has of his subordinates will determine his management behaviour. Those two aspects are always linked. A manager's behaviour, however, evokes a reaction from his subordinates that "proves" his assumptions to be correct. He therefore continues to manage them in what he considers to be the "appropriate" style, not realising that his management behaviour is reinforcing those characteristics of his subordinates.

What is the yardstick for determining a manager's leadership abilities? If, for example, we wanted to assess the leadership qualities of a cabinet minister, what would we look at? Certainly not the type of speech he gives in parliament. We would look at the effectiveness of the government department under his control – and for some cabinet ministers that would be a rather uncomfortable yardstick.

How would we evaluate a clergyman's leadership skills? Certainly not from the sermon he preaches (although that is also important). No, we would look at the spiritual depth of his congregation – and for some clergymen that would be an uncomfortable yardstick.

How would we assess a manager's leadership abilities? Not by looking at his technical competence (although he certainly must have that), but by assessing the competence of his subordinates. That means simply that managers who are always complaining about the poor employees they are stuck with are telling us something about their own leadership.

Part 3
Motivating subordinates

6 THE ESSENCE OF MOTIVATION

What is "motivation"?

The word "motivation" is used freely by many people, yet it may not always be very clear what is really meant by "motivating a subordinate". Does it mean getting him to work harder, or to put in longer hours, or to show more initiative?

The most common answer given by managers when asked to define motivation is: "Influencing a subordinate to achieve the goal that the manager wants him to achieve." One might add that he has to achieve that goal efficiently, while another will say the subordinate has to *want* to do it. In essence motivation is seen as getting someone to do something. Does that sound like a good definition of motivation? Let's try it out:

> If I want my dog out of the house, I can yell at him and kick him, and he will go outside. Am I motivating the dog? After all, he has done what I wanted him to do.
>
> Most managers will agree that that is not really motivation because the dog was "forced" to go outside against his will.
>
> What if I take a bone and lure the dog out? Now he has done what I wanted him to do of his own free will. Is this motivation? No, this is bribery.
>
> *I* wanted the dog to go outside, so *I* was the one who was motivated. The dog only *moved*.

To understand the concept of "motivation" in the management sense, it is essential to understand the difference between *movement* and *motivation*.

When a person carries out a task for the sake of remuneration, he is being *moved*.

He doesn't particularly like the work that he has to perform but he is willing to do it for the sake of what he can get for doing it.

> Very few students are motivated to study. The majority are *moved* to study. They do not enjoy putting in long hours of mental effort, but they are willing to do it for the sake of what they can get for doing it, namely some kind of qualification in the form of a degree or a diploma.
> In the same way very few school leavers are truly motivated to seek employment. They are *moved* to look for work because they need an income in order to live.

My involvement with commerce and industry has led me to believe that the majority of employees are in the position of being moved to carry out their tasks rather than motivated.

Many of the incentive schemes aimed at "motivating" employees are simply efforts to "move" them. For example, when the manager tells his staff that they can go home as soon as a particular task is completed, it is amazing how quickly the job can be done. This is a typical example of movement. The workers will increase their work pace, not because they like what they are doing, but because they want the free time. In the same way most financial incentive schemes are simply attempts to "move" employees to produce more. It's nothing but a "carrot" that is dangled in front of their noses.

It is important to understand that it is not wrong to move subordinates. Managers have been doing it for centuries, either from behind or from the front. Moving them from behind involves threatening workers with some dire consequence (e.g. the "five-point plan"). Moving workers from the front implies offering them all kinds of benefits (like promotion, salary increase, bonus, etc.) to induce them to perform better. But it still remains movement, not motivation. It was Frederick Herzberg (1968a:53-62) who coined the term "KITA" (for "Kick in the . . . ") in an article on the process of moving subordinates.

What then is motivation in the management context? What gives subordinates that extra commitment and dedication? The answer is relatively simple:

When a person carries out a task because he *enjoys* doing it, he is being *motivated*.

This simple definition highlights the fact that real dedication and commitment can come only when the *task content* is enjoyable to the worker.

> Many people spend a great deal of time and effort completing crossword puzzles. They receive no remuneration for this, and most of them do not bother to submit completed puzzles in the hope of winning a prize.
>
> When asked why they devote so much of their valuable time to an activity for which they earn nothing, the answer is usually: "Because I *like* it."
>
> That is an example of *motivation*.

Much of the confusion over the issue of motivation arises because there is no clear distinction between "motivation" and "movement". For example, the argument about whether money can motivate employees is confusing. It would be more appropriate to ask whether money can get someone to do something – and the answer is undoubtedly "yes". However, can money get a worker to *enjoy* his task more? The answer to that is probably "no", because the task content hasn't changed.

The key to motivating subordinates, therefore, lies in making the tasks of the workers so "enjoyable" that they will be keen to carry them out.

However, before discussing what a manager needs to do to make the work of his staff more enjoyable, there is another concept that needs to be clarified.

The opposite of "unhappy"

When we ask someone what the opposite of "unhappy" is, the answer is almost always "happy". I question that. When I sprained my ankle, I hobbled around in pain for a few days. That made me very unhappy, but when my ankle was in fine shape again, it didn't make me happy. In fact, I never think about my ankles unless they hurt. No, the opposite of "unhappy" is simply "not unhappy". It's a kind of neutral feeling.

When my wife comes home with a new dress and asks me what I think of it, I can give her one of three answers (after I've found out how much it costs). I can tell her it looks terrific, I can tell her that it doesn't suit her, or I can respond the way most husbands do and tell her it's "okay". When I tell her that it's "not too bad", I'm telling her that I neither like it nor dislike it. I just feel neutral about it. I am "not unhappy".

In the same way the opposite of "happy" is simply "not happy" and the same neutral feeling is implied.

This is not just a play on words. Herzberg (1968b) highlighted some very significant implications relating to job satisfaction: "If there are aspects in the work situation that make employees unhappy, it will not give them job satisfaction if these aspects are corrected or improved." It will only make them "not unhappy".

> Every now and then we read in the media that civil servants (including university lecturers) are highly dissatisfied with their remuneration. Then after a period of agitation and negotiation the government announces a considerable pay increase for all its employees.
> Do the civil servants work harder after receiving such an increase? No, they only complain less.

This reaction is certainly not limited to civil servants. It applies to virtually all employees. For example, people can become extremely dissatisfied if they sense that they are being treated unfairly; yet treating all employees fairly in no way guarantees that they will enjoy the work that they have to do.

Three levels of performance

All employees function at one of three basic levels and most managers have had to deal with subordinates who functioned at each of these three levels.

Minimum level	–	Expected level	–	Maximum level
Doing less than expected		Carrying out duties faithfully		Doing more than expected

Examples of the *minimum* level would be employees who regularly arrive late for work (and make up for it by leaving early). They dodge work, make numerous mistakes, turn in poor quality work, take their full sick leave every year, and even steal company property.

The in-between level is the *expected* level where a worker does only what is required of him – nothing more and nothing less. "A fair day's work for a fair day's pay."

When workers function at the *maximum* level, they often arrive early and leave late, put in extra work (unpaid overtime), use their own initiative, etc. Performance at the maximum level, however, will occur only when job incumbents find the task content enjoyable, that is, when they like what they are doing.

> To illustrate the concept that employees are motivated by the *task itself*, let's take the case of a qualified engineer being offered the job of toilet cleaner with an organisation that has the most marvellous personnel policies and fringe benefits. The atmosphere in the organisation is one of supportive friendliness, the working conditions are superb (all the toilets are made of genuine Italian marble), the job is ranked at a high status with the official title of "sanitation engineer", there is guaranteed job security, the working hours are pleasant, and the pay is three times higher than that of any engineering position he could get elsewhere.
>
> Would he take the position of toilet cleaner? Perhaps.
>
> But at what level would he function? Most probably at the *expected* level. It is very unlikely that he would put in extra effort or do more than is expected of him because the task of cleaning toilets could never be enjoyable for someone with his level of education. He will, therefore, not function at the maximum level. Neither will he function at the minimum level, because his conscience will bother him. His attitude is likely to be that "since the company treats me so well, I will at least do what is expected of me".

The implications

What does this all mean for management? The implication is that managers have to do two things to motivate their subordinates. In the first place they have to make sure that there is no cause for job dissatisfaction – but that by itself is not sufficient since employees will then only function at the expected level. Management must, secondly, take specific steps to create job satisfaction for their subordinates, for only then will they function at the maximum level.

7 PREVENTING JOB DISSATISFACTION

A prerequisite for motivation

It is very difficult to make workers excited about their work if they are unhappy about their working conditions. Some of these issues may be very obvious (e.g. low wages). However, in most cases management is not even aware of the things that cause such dissatisfaction – even though to employees they are extremely important. Albert Koopman (1987:28) refers to these factors as "tea and coffee" issues that must be dealt with before there can be any talk of commitment and dedication.

Many issues refer to situations that are taken for granted by management, but are seen by the subordinates as a form of discrimination. Koopman lists a number of typical issues that were causing dissatisfaction in his own company, particularly among the black staff. Some of the questions they asked were these:

☐ "Why do the whites in the firm get a half-day off, but not the blacks?"
☐ "Why do the senior staff get steak and chips during stocktaking while the junior staff have to settle for hamburgers?"
☐ "If we're five minutes late, the boss docks our pay. Why doesn't he notice when we work ten minutes overtime?"
☐ "Why do the blacks have tea in mugs when the whites drink out of cups?"
☐ "Why do some people get off on stocktaking days while we are forced to stay?"

Koopman points out that these are not political issues; nor are they aggressive questions. They are simply issues relating to basic human dignity. If management denies that there is a problem or retaliates in an aggressive manner, the source of dissatisfaction will not be removed. Subordinates will learn to keep quiet, but management must not be surprised if their attempts to generate loyalty and commitment fail dismally.

Sources of dissatisfaction

The greatest source of dissatisfaction among workers seems to stem from the way they are *treated*. Every worker expects to be treated well. Surveys reveal that most subordinates, regardless of their positions in the organisation, have three basic expectations concerning the way in which they would like to be treated by management:
- "Provide me with favourable working conditions."
- "Maintain a pleasant relationship with me."
- "Deal with me fairly."

If these expectations are not met, all attempts at motivating employees can fall by the board. Furthermore, if workers *think* that management is giving them a raw deal, they will respond accordingly, regardless of the actual situation.

Favourable working conditions

These include such things as good equipment, sound procedures, adequate working space, reasonable working hours, good pay, favourable fringe benefits, etc. If these are perceived to be inadequate, a tremendous amount of dissatisfaction and resentment can be created.

> A library was moved to a new building. When I asked a senior librarian how she liked the new building, she expressed a great deal of distress over the fact that in the old building she had her own office. In the new building she was placed in an open-plan office with a number of other members of staff. Despite her many years of service, she was seriously thinking of resigning.

Dissatisfaction can be aroused by petty rules and regulations. Bureaucratic procedures often "motivate" employees to try to beat the system.

The story is told of an employee who lost his raincoat while on a business trip. When he claimed for it as part of his travelling expenses, the accountant disallowed the claim. When he returned from his next trip, he submitted his claim with a little note that said: "The raincoat is included somewhere in these figures; see if you can find it."

The sad part is that rules very seldom contribute to the efficient running of an organisation. Many of them serve only to annoy employees.

> An engineer in a very large government corporation told me of his frustrations whenever he needed to purchase equipment or materials. He had to fill in a lengthy requisition form (in triplicate), get at least three senior managers to sign it, and by the time he finally got it, he "no longer needed it".
>
> One day he was so fed up with the system that as a joke he submitted a requisition for an Impala jet fighter – in triplicate and all.
>
> He forgot all about it until a month or so later the warehouse manager phoned to say: "I have an approved order for an Impala jet, but don't know where to buy one."
>
> So much for signatures!

The issue that probably causes more unhappiness at the work-place than anything else is *money*. If employees feel that they are not being paid enough, they are going to be extremely unhappy, and the chances are good that any effort to motivate them will be met with a great deal of resistance. It is essential that employees should be seen to be remunerated fairly and adequately for the work that they do. This vital topic is discussed more fully at a later stage.

Pleasant relationships

Employees expect to be treated like human beings. Managers must be aware of the individual needs of their subordinates and learn to treat them with consideration. Nobody wants to be shouted at or treated as if he is inferior. Nobody wants to be humiliated in front of his fellow workers. Nobody wants to be talked down to.

> It is ironical that managers who insist on being addressed formally by their subordinates are often less respected than those managers who relate to their subordinates on an informal person-to-person basis.

Treating subordinates with respect and consideration is one of the most basic requirements for any manager – yet so many seem to be under the impression that a position of authority gives them the right to lord it over their staff, perhaps because of their own feelings of inferiority. However, in the process they end up as failures as far as the management of people is concerned.

> A memo was sent by the national service manager of a company to all the regional service managers under his control:
> "I will not tolerate incompetence in any shape or form . . . Any instruction from a superior must be carried out, however onerous you may consider it to be . . . The most severe action will be taken against anyone who exhibits any of the following: negative attitude, ignorance, disobeying instructions, or lack of discipline. If you have any of the above traits, change them now, or I will."
> That is the quickest way to quash all thinking, all initiative, and all motivation.
> The organisation lost some very good employees as a result of this manager's attitude, while many of his subordinates deliberately started "sabotaging" him.
> That company's performance took a serious nosedive, until the manager was eventually fired.

Surveys to establish the morale of employees in specific organisations frequently highlight "poor relationships with the boss" as the major source of discontent. This is especially common in South Africa, where the manager/subordinate relationship is further complicated by the white/black relationship.

> A nation-wide strike in one of South Africa's largest companies originated when a white supervisor scolded a black subordinate in a humiliating manner in front of his fellow workers for some petty offence.
> The subordinate (who, as it turned out, was not guilty of the offence) replied in a sarcastic tone of voice. This infuriated the supervisor to such an extent that he fired the "offender". This eventually resulted in a strike which cost over R60 million in lost production.
> Some supervisor!

Fair dealings

Closely related to the problem of poor relationships is the question of unfairness. When an employee thinks that he is being discriminated against, it creates resentment and a strong desire to get back at management. A worker may feel that he is being treated unfairly if, for example:
- a fellow worker doing the same type of work is earning more than he is;
- he is reprimanded for an offence while someone else committing the same offence gets off scot-free;
- the boss makes a promise that "he will look into a matter" but conveniently forgets about it;
- he gets the same merit increase as a fellow worker who is a known loafer;
- he is overlooked for promotion and management gives him some feeble excuse.

This kind of management behaviour will create a tremendous amount of distrust between boss and subordinates and will neutralise any attempt to motivate them.

> At a large timber company a group of managers was involved in a "one hundred day" project to solve a particular problem. The regional manager promised them a weekend at the Wild Coast with their wives if they completed the project successfully.
>
> They literally worked day and night, but when the project was finally completed, the regional manager came with a lame excuse that head office had refused to approve the weekend excursion.
>
> As a result, the attitude of most team members was: "That's the last time I will ever work on a project."

Peter Drucker (1974:462), a well-known management consultant in the United States, says that subordinates will tolerate a manager's mistakes, but not his lack of integrity. If his subordinates no longer trust him, a manager may as well resign and look for another position. Albert Koopman (1987:45) also stresses the fact that his management team had to devote a great deal of effort to gaining the confidence and trust of their employees before they could obtain any kind of commitment from them.

The farmer in Natal who was given the special productivity award (see chapter 4) spent months on improving his relationship with his workers before he was in a position to start motivating them. For example, he made a point of writing down every promise he made to ensure that he kept his word promptly – even on simple issues like telling them that he would order some materials that they were asking for.

The importance of fair labour practices cannot be overemphasised. Every organisation should, for example, follow a disciplinary code that is not only understood by the workers, but also seen to be fair. It is not for nothing that unions place so much emphasis on the fair treatment of their members – and our labour legislation backs them all the way.

What is good treatment?

How does management know that its conditions are adequate and that the employees are getting a fair deal? The answer lies in the fact that dissatisfaction stems from *comparisons*.

> An employee may be quite satisfied with his pay until he compares it with that of someone whom he regards as his equal. If it compares unfavourably, he will be very dissatisfied, regardless of what he earns.
>
> Of course, if it compares favourably, he doesn't think the other person is being treated unfairly – he simply rationalises in his own mind that he deserves to be earning more.

When it comes to determining an adequate working environment, management should not go overboard. All they need to do is to make sure that their remuneration package, their fringe benefits, their working facilities, their working hours, etc. are *comparable* with those offered by other comparable organisations. To provide more may attract more job applicants, but it will not necessarily lead to higher employee productivity because it won't make the task more enjoyable.

> Salary surveys by reputable management consultants can supply useful information to enable management to keep up with the conditions in the labour market.

Another indication that the expectations of employees are not being met is a high labour turnover. The large number of resignations in the teaching community, for example, is a sure indication of the dissatisfaction in the teaching profession.

Complaints and grievances are also good barometers of the general morale of the worker corps. I'm not suggesting that managers must jump every time one of their workers is unhappy about something. The "professional gripers" will always be with us, and it is best to ignore them or get rid of them – as long as management is convinced that the employees have *no valid reason* to be dissatisfied.

The result of good treatment

Not all managers are guilty of the kind of behaviour that I have described. There are many organisations that provide favourable working conditions, with managers who treat their employees decently and fairly – yet they still find that their labour productivity is not what it could be.

The reason is easy to find. Good treatment will not motivate employees to perform better, because it does not affect the task content – it does not make the task more enjoyable. A typical example is that of the engineer cleaning toilets (see chapter 6). His working conditions were absolutely superb, yet he performed at the expected level because the task was not an enjoyable one.

If employees are treated badly, however, they will function at the minimum level and feel perfectly justified in doing so.

> A young farm manager told me that he had worked for a particular farmer, but could not last longer than three months because of "the labour situation".
>
> The farmer used to beat his farm workers physically if they did not perform their work satisfactorily. Now he is getting too old to do that, so he just throws bricks at them.
>
> The result? The sabotage on the farm was rife. There was frequently sand in the diesel, fences were cut, animals went missing, etc.

Treat employees badly and they will perform badly. However, treating them well does not necessarily mean that they will perform well. The best possible treatment a manager can give his subordinates will never get them to do more than what is expected of them. To motivate subordinates to function at the maximum level, a manager has to make the tasks of his subordinates enjoyable to them. How managers can achieve this is discussed in the following chapters.

8 CREATING JOB SATISFACTION

The key ingredient

What makes work enjoyable? What makes workers look forward to getting on with the task? What kind of task motivates subordinates? The answer to these questions is relatively simple. It all boils down to one key ingredient and that is *pride*. Unless the accomplishment of a task brings about a feeling of pride, the person doing it will never be motivated.

It should not be a conceited pride that makes him think he is better than others, but rather a feeling of something "well done", feeling good about his abilities and proud of what he has accomplished. Unless managers can learn to arouse in their subordinates that feeling of self-esteem, their chances of motivating them will be slim indeed.

> Travelling from Johannesburg, I passed a group of workers who were cutting grass at the side of the highway. They were working at a snail's pace, and my initial reaction was: "Look at those loafers! Isn't that just typical?"
>
> But as I thought about them, I wondered if they could ever go home at the end of a day with a feeling of accomplishment. Each worker was just a number, one of many. He had no responsibility whatsoever and it was not even possible to identify whether he had done a good job or not.
>
> What could he be proud of? Stealing a jacket from a motor car, and getting away with it, would at least give him something to feel "proud" about.

External versus internal stimulus

Movement as defined in chapter 6 has to do with external stimuli. It is nothing other than the classic "carrot and stick" approach, where workers are offered some kind of reward for doing certain things. *Motivation*, on the other hand, has to do with an internal stimulus, because those feelings of pride and self-esteem can only come from within.

Animals also respond to the "carrot and stick" approach, and if management relies only on external stimuli to "move" their employees, they are treating them like animals – and most people treat their animals well. However, human beings differ from animals in the fact that every person, regardless of colour or creed, has a basic need to be proud of himself, to have self-respect.

Moving a subordinate is like putting a battery inside him. It has to be recharged constantly from the outside. If an employee is unhappy about his pay, a good salary increase will make him "not unhappy" – but sooner or later he will become dissatisfied again. If an army officer is unhappy with his rank, a promotion will solve that – but only for a relatively short time. He is going to become unhappy again. That is human nature.

Motivating a subordinate, however, is like giving him his own built-in generator. He generates his own power, because it focuses on the sense of pride and self-esteem that comes from within. What's more, it has a long-term effect. Most employees have difficulty in remembering improvements in working conditions that were introduced a year or two ago – yet they have no difficulty in remembering things they achieved ten or twenty years ago. And when they think back on those achievements, they still experience a glow of satisfaction and pride.

The role of pride

Let me illustrate the role of pride in stimulating the desired behaviour in people.

> One of the major headaches farmers are faced with is the fact that workers often come to work on a Monday morning under the influence of alcohol. Scolding them and punishing them have not solved the problem.
> One farmer, however, did solve the problem. A few years ago he started instilling a sense of pride in his workers (and that was an important first step).
> When some of his workers arrived "under the weather" at work

53

> one day, he called all his staff together and told them that he did not mind them drinking over weekends – or during the week for that matter – but if they got up in the morning with their heads spinning, they were to stay at home, and somebody else would do their work for them. However, he would pay them their full wages. Even if they stayed at home for several days, he would pay them in full and not reprimand them, but they were not to come to work.
>
> When he first told me of this approach, I told him he must be crazy, even though I had taught him the basics of motivation. Yet in the last few years he has not had a single worker drunk at work or drunk at home. There is too much pride at stake.
>
> The problem has been completely solved!

If that was an isolated incident, I would regard it as an exception, but there have been a number of such cases all over South Africa. A farmer in the Western Transvaal told me that he had given two of his farm workers a task that would require at least two days to complete. On the morning of the first day he went to see how they were progressing. The area where they were working was downhill, so he switched off his engine and free-wheeled to the work site, where he found them sleeping.

They were expecting the usual "five-point plan", but since he had recently attended one of my seminars, he just said to them: "Don't sleep over there where your overalls will get dirty; sleep on the grass where they won't get dirty," and he drove off. By seven o'clock that evening the task was done.

Such incidents are not limited to the farming scene. A factory manager on the East Rand told me that he had applied the same approach with one of his workers. He had sent him home "until he was well enough to work again". Not only did the subordinate refuse to go home; to date he has not committed that offence again.

Why do workers respond in this way? Surely they will abuse such soft handling? I can best answer that with a comment from a black warehouse supervisor.

> This supervisor from Tzaneen has been very successful in applying the human resource theory. It was with great pride that he took me on a tour of the warehouse and told me of all the things he had done to motivate his staff.

He then told me of one worker who was known as "the beer king" because he was often under the influence of alcohol. The supervisor had tried everything to get him to stop, but nothing had helped. Of course, he could have fired him, but he was a very good worker when sober.

Finally, the supervisor told him in front of all the other workers to stay at home for a full week so that he could have enough time to drink and said that he would still be paid his full wages.

Four months later there was still no sign of any drunkenness, and what's more, that worker has since used his own initiative to bring about quite a few improvements in the warehouse – and he is very proud of this.

I expressed my surprise to the supervisor at the fact that his approach had worked so well. When I suggested that a worker would surely abuse such a "privilege", his answer was: "No, Sir, he cannot enjoy his money if he has not worked for it."

I think he would make a good psychologist!

Creating an emotional obligation

When employees are not punished for committing an offence, it creates a sense of shame and puts the individual under an emotional obligation. (That's why many teenagers would rather be punished for their misbehaviour than to have dad say to them: "I'm disappointed in you.") However, penalising the offender cancels out the obligation, and seldom leads to an improvement in behaviour.

One manager warned a subordinate that every time he came to work under the influence of alcohol, he would deduct R2 from his wages.

The first time he arrived drunk, R2 was taken off. The second time another R2 was deducted. The third time he staggered towards the manager and said: "Bosshh, here'shh my R2."

What the manager had in fact done in threatening to deduct R2 was to imply that it was okay for the worker to come to work drunk, as long as he paid R2 for the privilege of doing so.

The punishment did not bring about a change in behaviour – it only increased the price of his liquor.

Of course, some managers have a very simple solution to this problem of drinking. Any employee found to be under the weather is dismissed summarily. This works well, until his best worker, whose services he really needs, arrives at work sozzled. What does he do then?

Creating an emotional obligation is a very important concept that is easily overlooked by management. There is a generally accepted belief that everything can be compensated for with money.

> At a forestry plantation in the Northern Transvaal fires would break out from time to time, and it was expected of the entire work force to come to help fight the fire, even on weekends – which they did.
>
> However, management felt that the workers should be paid overtime if they helped with fire-fighting in their off-time. That, after all, was only fair.
>
> The next time a fire broke out, only a third of the labour force came to help. The others stayed at home. They were willing to forego their overtime pay for the privilege of staying at home. By offering them overtime pay management had actually cancelled out the emotional obligation to help fight forest fires.

It is not a healthy approach to reward a worker with money every time he does something extra. Money has an insulting element in it. (That's why we feel insulted if a friend offers to pay us for a favour we have done for him.)

Good performance should be rewarded financially at the end of a year – and that is discussed in chapter 17 – but when subordinates are given extra money every time they do something well, they are deprived of a sense of accomplishment and satisfaction.

> Of course there are workers who have come to expect a tip whenever they do something extra for us, but their pride has usually been downtrodden to such an extent that they have no self-respect left.

Schoolchildren are no different

I came across this concept of focusing on self-esteem when I spent a year teaching at a school in Buenos Aires, Argentina. It was a private school where the pupils attended classes in English in the morning, and in Spanish in the afternoon. However, at the end of the year they passed (or failed) on their work in the Spanish classes, not the English classes.

That meant that I could not fail anybody; nor was I allowed to spank a pupil if he didn't do his schoolwork. I couldn't give extra homework as punishment since they seldom did their normal homework. I could not keep the pupils in after hours, since they had to attend the Spanish classes and after that it was too late. Sending them to the headmaster didn't help either, since he was a kind old gentleman who spoke nicely to the boys and then sent them back to class.

I was extremely frustrated because I had no way of forcing my pupils to study. Shouting at them didn't have much effect. The only "punishment" I could mete out was to send a pupil who misbehaved out of the classroom – but at one stage there were more pupils *outside* the classroom than inside. I later discovered that they were actually taking bets to see who would be kicked out first. My teaching was not exactly successful, although the pupils seemed to have great fun.

Then during the first school vacation I saw the film "To Sir, with love" – and I strongly recommend that every teacher should see this film or read the book. As a result of that film I decided to change my entire approach. I walked into a standard 8 maths class on the first day of the next term and said to 23 boys: "I won't know any more maths at the end of the year than I know now. I am not here for my benefit but for yours. I will go out of my way to help anyone who wants to study maths, but if you don't want to, you don't have to. From now on you may do anything you like in my class. You may do other homework, read comics, even play cards. The only restriction is that you may not cause a disturbance." They whispered among themselves and then all put their heads down on their desks and pretended to go to sleep. Although I was fuming, I calmly said: "Anybody for maths?" and then sat down at my table and read a novel. (Frankly, I didn't know what else to do.)

After five minutes they stood around the table and told me that they had only been joking – they wanted to carry on with the lesson. So we did. Five of the boys opted to drop out, but all the others started working. I made it very clear that homework was entirely voluntary, and in the beginning when some did not do it (to test me, I presume), I treated them in exactly the same way as everybody else. The result was that they all did their homework every time, since it was no longer any fun to try to outwit the teacher. Unwittingly I had touched their pride and it led to a group of eighteen highly motivated pupils. (I doubt if I would have succeeded in making the other five study – even if I had tried to "force" them.)

> Parents do their children a great disservice by forcing them to do their homework. They are actually taking away their sense of responsibility. When mother insists and checks that the homework is done every day, *she* becomes responsible for her child's schoolwork – and the child becomes irresponsible.
>
> Thousands of mothers across the country pass standards 1, 2, 3, etc. year in and year out, and in the process they deprive their children of an important sense of achievement.

Some key considerations

What about the role of money?

Why do so many organisations have monetary incentive schemes? Why do so many employees (and unions) emphasise money? Surely it plays a vital part in motivating subordinates?

Money is important! If employees feel that they are not being paid enough, they are going to function at the minimum level. Furthermore, money can *move* people – there is no doubt about that! But it does not move everybody. The overall effectiveness of incentive schemes has been rather limited. The reason is that managers have relied on the offer of money to provide the inner driving force and money cannot do that.

> In one section of a manufacturing company, eight workers were involved in folding the boxes in which the products were to be packed. They were told that each one had to fold twenty batches a day, but that they would be paid x cents for every batch they folded over and above twenty. This was a typical incentive scheme; yet the average production was less than twenty batches a day.
>
> Shortly after his return from a seminar the manager had to keep

an eye on these workers because their supervisor was sick. So he decided to try out some of my ideas. He told them that he wanted to see how good they were, and asked each one to tell him how many batches he thought he could fold. The answers ranged from 21 to 25 batches.

At the end of the day all the workers had exceeded their goals and the manager made a point of praising them and asking them to set new goals for the following day. Again the goals were exceeded.

When the supervisor returned the next day, he advised him to continue with the system. Within a few days the supervisor informed the manager that he had transferred four of the workers to another section "because there was insufficient storage space!"

The remaining four folders maintained their high performance level, folding up to sixty batches a day – and being paid for it, because the original incentive scheme was still in force.

What had made the difference? In both situations money was offered for extra effort. Why did it work in the second situation but not in the first? The answer lies in the management approach. In the first situation management relied on the offer of money to provide the driving force. In the second situation management relied on the creation of pride and a sense of achievement. The money was a secondary issue.

When I first heard that story, it somehow put the whole question of money and incentive schemes into perspective. Some incentive schemes are so ingrained that I doubt if they will ever be changed. Salesmen (in the majority of cases) will always expect to be paid a commission. That is not necessarily wrong. The mistake that sales managers must avoid, however, is to think that the offer of commission is sufficient reward. No matter how much salesmen earn, they still need to be given recognition and praise for exceeding their targets, landing a big contract, etc.

Can money ever be used to motivate subordinates? It can, when it is given as recognition for achievement. The greatest motivational impact from money is obtained when it is given *over and above the obligation of the manager* to those who have performed exceptionally well. I stress that management should not be under an obligation to give it; then it is seen as the employee's "right" and it loses its motivational impact.

> Promising employees some kind of fixed-formula bonus in the hope that they will perform better is the same as treating them like circus animals.
> If they perform their little "trick", they will get their "lump of sugar".

Employees may be aware of the fact that good performance will be rewarded financially at the end of the year, but the actual amount should always be left to the discretion of management. As soon as a certain amount is promised, it changes the "reward" element into a "right".

What about the importance of job security?

Job security for all employees is very important to prevent job dissatisfaction. People who are under constant threat of being fired will be "moved" to do what is required of them, but there will be no commitment on their part. They will continually be on the lookout for other employment and will devote a good deal of energy to "outwitting the boss" and doing just enough not to get fired. Every employee needs to have job security.

> A factory in Isando retrenched 42 workers following a drop in sales turnover. When business picked up again, most of them were re-employed, but it had a tremendously negative effect on all the employees.
> The workers were deliberately restricting production out of fear that if they produced more, some of them would again be retrenched.
> Management found it extremely difficult to motivate their workers in such a climate.

However, job security will not motivate employees, since it does not affect the *enjoyment* of the task. If it did, all government officials (and university lecturers) would be highly motivated.

What about the attractiveness of fringe benefits?

A company car? Recreational facilities? Long vacations? Overseas trips? A housing subsidy? Do these factors not motivate employees?

The answer is negative. Such benefits may attract job applicants, but they will not motivate them.

> Many years ago I had job offers from two companies. Both jobs seemed attractive, but I finally joined the company that offered a hundred per cent housing loan that would enable me to purchase my own house.
> However, I worked hard in that job because I was given a good deal of responsibility, not because I had a housing loan. I took that for granted as my right.

How important is status?

Status in terms of job titles (calling the toilet cleaner a "sanitation engineer") or special privileges (a bigger company car, a bigger office, reserved parking, etc.) will not motivate anybody because it does not affect the task content.

Often status is seen as a motivator because people who have high status in an organisation tend to be more motivated than people who have low status. The reason for that does not lie with the status itself, but with the responsibility that usually accompanies higher status.

> In an organisation like a university where lecturing staff have different levels of status (from a junior lecturer to a professor) there is often not much difference in the level of motivation, since the task content remains basically the same.

Status can, however, be a strong source of dissatisfaction. If an employee feels that his rank in the organisation is too low for the level of responsibility he is carrying – especially when he compares himself with some of his peers – he will in all probability be very unhappy.

The principle is very straightforward. The *task environment* must compare favourably if job dissatisfaction among the staff is to be avoided, but job satisfaction can be obtained only when the *task content* becomes a source of pride for the worker.

What stimulates pride in a worker?

These principles may all sound very well in theory, but what about the practical situation? How can a manager stimulate pride in a lowly toilet cleaner? Surely there are some jobs that simply don't lend themselves to this approach?

I believe not. By that I am not implying that *anybody* can be motivated to do *any* job. It would be very difficult to motivate an engineer to clean toilets. But it is possible to motivate an unskilled worker to be a good toilet cleaner. The assumption I am making is that the people filling specific positions are educationally matched for those positions. There are unskilled workers doing low-level work, semi-skilled workers functioning as machine operators and skilled workers as artisans (or matriculants in clerical jobs, graduates in professional positions, etc.).

On this assumption most employees (90 per cent of the work force) can be motivated if their jobs provide them with one or more of the following elements:
☐ A sense of achievement
☐ Responsibility for decision making
☐ Recognition of achievement

The emphasis should, therefore, fall on the *task content*. How to build those elements into the tasks of subordinates is the subject of the next three chapters.

9 A SENSE OF ACHIEVEMENT

The key element

What can a manager do to the task of a subordinate so that it will give him a sense of achievement? The answer is quite simple. The key to giving someone a sense of achievement is to *measure* that achievement. If performance is not measured, how will the manager and/or his subordinate know that the goal has been achieved?

> To tell a truck driver "to look after his vehicle" is a waste of time, since it will be very difficult to assess when he has accomplished this.
>
> However, to tell a truck driver what the running costs of his vehicle have been in the past and to ask him whether he can improve on them is creating a basis whereby a goal can be set with respect to his running costs.
>
> Every time he achieves the target, he is very likely to experience a sense of achievement.

In their very exciting book *The winning way*, authors Ball and Asbury (1989:39) highlight the fact that many of South Africa's top companies have achieved excellent results because they have gone to the trouble of measuring those results.

I stand amazed at how often managers tell their subordinates what they must *do*, instead of what they must *achieve*. The focus is so often on the *activities* of their workers, instead of on their *end results*.

Activity or end result?

Some years ago the superintendent at a hospital asked a colleague to lend him a pair of binoculars to take to the game reserve. When the colleague brought them to the office the next day, the superintendent looked out of his sixth floor window to test them. To his surprise he saw a group of gardeners sitting under a tree. This was of particular interest to him since the gardening department was one of the departments under his control.

He checked every ten minutes or so, and after an hour called their supervisor to his office, where he proceeded to reprimand him severely for "not exercising adequate control over his staff" and for "not knowing what his subordinates were up to".

The next day this supervisor came to consult me about what he could do to motivate his gardeners. He explained that the hospital grounds were quite large and that he was always running around telling his eighteen gardeners what to do, checking up on their work, seeing that they had the right materials, etc. It was impossible for him to check on his staff every minute of the day, and he felt that his boss was extremely unfair in calling him incompetent.

My first question was to ask him whether his gardeners were competent.

> That is an important consideration. If employees do not know how to do a task properly, they cannot be motivated – they need to be trained.
>
> A large car manufacturing plant at Rosslyn has achieved tremendous success in motivating their assembly line workers – but they spent the first year or two drawing up detailed training manuals and they ensured that each operator knew exactly how to execute his task correctly.
>
> When we talk of motivating subordinates, I am assuming, therefore, that they are people who have been adequately trained.

He assured me that they had been with him for quite a number of years and that they knew what had to be done.

I suggested to him that he divide the hospital grounds into eighteen sections, allocating one section to each gardener. He should tell them that they could come to work when they liked, go home when they liked, and even sleep when they liked. The only thing he would do was to inspect their sections once a week and give them a rating out of 10 to indicate how well they had worked. A rating of 3 would be considered adequate, that is, the expected level. (A rating of 2 would mean "poor" and a rating of 1 would be "useless".) That left plenty of scope between 3 and 10 for improvement.

That was the only "management training" he received from me, but three weeks later he proudly came to show me his rating book. He was amazed at the positive reaction from his workers. Instead of arriving late and leaving early, many of them were coming to work early and leaving late. The pride that they took in their sections was obvious to see. Some had even come to thank him for the fact that he was now recording in a book how good they were.

> Good performers always welcome being measured because they want to know that the boss knows how good they are.
> It is usually the poor performers who resist attempts to measure their performance. They always come up with some excuse or another as to why the measurement is unfair or not applicable to them.

Four years later the system was still in operation. The real point of the story, however, was three months after the incident when the supervisor went back to the superintendent and explained the whole system to him. He then said an amazingly courageous thing to his boss. "Sir, if you see any section of these grounds in poor shape, please call me in. But, if you see any of my staff standing around idle, with all due respect, Sir, it's got nothing to do with you."

He was right. It does not matter whether gardeners are busy or not. What matters is an attractive garden. That's the end result.

Teaching subordinates to look busy

So many managers have a hang-up about their workers having to be busy – but in the process they teach their subordinates to *look* busy when the boss is in view. Most workers in South Africa have developed that skill to a fine art.

> A factory manager in Isando told me that one of their directors arrived unannounced from head office, walked through the plant and blasted anybody who was not "busy".

He did that on only two occasions. Thereafter the security guard at the entrance gate was given strict instructions to phone through the minute the director arrived. With a few well-placed whistles everybody was warned and the director never had occasion to scold anybody again.

He is absolutely convinced of the effectiveness of his management style, but the factory workers are laughing behind his back.

What reason does a worker have for doing a good job? Why should he keep costs to a minimum? Why should he increase his production rate? Why should he be careful to avoid mistakes? Most employees do not have a good reason. The only time they will make some effort to be careful is when the boss is watching.

When their results are measured, however, it provides a very strong reason for wanting to achieve.

Motivating computer operators

Seven years of managing a computer operations department in a large international organisation was characterised by the manager constantly checking up on his subordinates and continually admonishing them to minimise their mistakes. Every time he took action to reduce the mistakes, the quality of the work improved but only for a short while.

When he returned from my management seminar, the manager called all his subordinates (who worked in three shifts) together and asked them to draw up a list of all the mistakes they had made in the past. He said he would come back to them, and decided that by subtracting 5 points per mistake from 100, he would be able to measure the performance of each shift.

He then went to the user departments and asked them to keep a record of each mistake that was made by the computer operators over a period of two weeks. He asked them not to tell his operators about this measurement, since he wanted to establish the current level of his department's service. He assured them that nobody would be reprimanded in any way.

At the end of two weeks he called another meeting of his staff and with the use of graphs presented them with the performance of each shift over those two weeks. The average was a score of 68,6. He then asked them if they considered this a fair reflection of their ability. This wounded their pride and they all agreed that they were capable of a higher score than that. After further discussion they agreed that a score of 85 was a fair standard. He told them that he would keep the score and give them feedback each week.

In the next six weeks they averaged a score of 94,0. When one of the shifts had a low score in one particular week, they immediately took the initiative to correct the problem themselves. They had a reason to want to perform well because their pride was at stake.

This system continued for at least four years, until the manager was promoted. I do not know if his successor continued with it, but in those four years they consistently maintained their high performance level.

> The question is often asked whether the operators do not get tired of the high performance after a while. The answer is negative. They no longer get as excited about their scores, but there is a general sense of satisfaction at being able to maintain such a high standard.
>
> The manager reported that whenever a shift's performance declined, he had only to ask something like: "What went wrong? That's not up to your usual standard," and the problem would be corrected in next to no time.
>
> He had learnt to appeal to their pride.

A cooling tower in record time

An outside contractor had taken eight months to erect a cooling tower for a large corporation in Natal. A year later another cooling tower was required in a hurry and management asked their own building and maintenance team whether they could do it.

The foreman called all his artisans together and planned each step in detail. They set a time schedule for each step and found to their surprise that the job could be done in nine weeks. The foreman expressed doubt as to whether they could do it and asked them to make sure that their calculations were correct. This was a real challenge to them to prove that they could do it.

They informed all the workers of the goals and put up a large poster at the site to indicate their progress towards achieving the goal. The workers developed such a keen interest that those who were absent for a day or two had to account to their colleagues why they were not at work – since they were "letting down the team". On several occasions the workers put in unpaid overtime in order to meet a deadline. They also went home early on some days when the interim target was reached.

The result? The cooling tower was completed five days earlier than planned. The job had been an exciting project because the workers could go home at the end of the day feeling proud of themselves.

What you measure is what you get

On a sugar cane estate on the South Coast of Natal the cane is transported during the day from the cane fields to various loading zones. At night the trucks from a transport company are loaded to take the cane to the sugar mill. The estate had a contract with the transport company that stipulated that if the average weight loaded during any one season was less than 27 tons, there would be an extra charge. Conversely, if the average load was more than 29 tons, there would be a discount.

At the end of the 1985 season the estate was presented with an account for more than R38 000 – the extra charge for underloaded trucks. If they had been a traditional management team, they would in all likelihood have scolded the loaders (and perhaps fired them), and appointed a white supervisor.

> In South Africa there is a commonly-held belief that it requires a white eye to keep a black body moving.

Instead, the estate management apologised to the loaders (a new management strategy?) for not telling them about the conditions of the contract and not informing them regularly how well they had loaded the trucks. They promised to provide each loading zone with a daily computer printout of the actual weight loaded, as soon as the figures were available from the mill.

The next year the figures for five of their loading zones were as follows:

	Zone 1	Zone 2	Zone 3	Zone 4	Zone 5
Av. tons	30,24	29,97	29,74	29,88	29,95

That year the transport company refunded them over R17 000 by way of discount. The year after that, however, they changed the contract because their drivers were getting too many traffic fines for overloaded vehicles.

"What you measure is what you get!"

Scolding is also a "measurement"

Managers often lose sight of the fact that a reprimand is also a form of measurement, since it conveys to the subordinate what aspects he is being assessed on.

At a brewery plant in the Transvaal an operator had to sit at the machine where cans were filled with beer. This was an automated process, but sometimes a can would fall over, setting up a chain reaction in which all the subsequent cans fell over. The operator's task was to stop the machine as quickly as possible, correct the problem and get the machine running again.

On several occasions, however, the supervisor scolded the operator for all the spilled beer and empty cans lying on the floor. The result was that each time a stoppage occurred he would spend about fifteen minutes cleaning the floor and getting rid of the cans before starting up the machine again. The delay in production time cost the company thousands – but at least there weren't any empty cans lying around.

Managers are constantly "measuring" the performance of their subordinates in one way or another – and what they "measure" is what they will get.

"Order placers" become "buyers"

In a large electronics factory in Pretoria, various production departments submit requisitions for materials to the purchasing department where the clerks then put the order through to the relevant supplier after checking that the details, authorisations, etc. are all in order.

The purchasing manager told me that he had always been a tyrant as far as his management style was concerned. He had drawn up detailed job descriptions and spent most of his time checking that his staff were following the correct procedures – his procedures. There was no room for his subordinates to use their initiative – a typical example of focusing on the activities and not on the end result.

The day after he came back from my seminar, he sat down with his four immediate subordinates and asked them to draw up their own goals. This took about three weeks of discussion and in the process a strong team spirit developed where his subordinates began to initiate their own ideas rather than responding to the ideas imposed on them.

It was eventually agreed that each buyer should be measured in terms of the following yardsticks:
☐ Percentage overdue items
☐ Number of mistakes per month
☐ Number of complaints from production departments
☐ Additional discounts negotiated

The result was that within six months the number of overdue items dropped from 19 per cent to 9 per cent. In the past the buyers had simply shrugged their shoulders when materials were not delivered on time – it was not their fault that the supplier was late. Now the buyers were putting pressure on the suppliers to meet their deadlines.

The mistakes in the department dropped from ten to five per month and the complaints dropped from ten written complaints a month (which always came via the factory manager) to the occasional verbal complaint from one of the production departments.

The buyers started squeezing the suppliers for extra discounts and during the first six months additional discounts totalling R40 582 were negotiated.

Suddenly issues such as discounts, customer satisfaction, mistakes and late deliveries became very important to the buyers, because their performance was being measured and their pride was at stake. The manager also reported that absenteeism had dropped considerably. His staff had become "buyers" and not just "order placers".

The most beautiful station in South Africa

A new station master was appointed to a fairly large railway station in the Northern Transvaal. The station was in a real mess. The weeds, bushes and run-down buildings created such a poor impression that even the regional manager of the SA Transport Services expressed doubt as to whether the place could ever be cleaned up.

However, the station master was a human resource manager. The first thing he did was to start regular meetings with all the staff to present them with the problems and discuss possible solutions. The first issue to be tackled was the appearance of the station. He allocated a specific section of the grounds to each worker (even to those who worked in the workshop and goods sheds) and asked each person to set a goal as to how long it would take to clean his section. The goal that was finally agreed on was six months.

Every week the station master inspected the work on each section and gave every worker a rating out of 5. They achieved their goal of cleaning up the place in exactly two months and twenty days.

He then challenged them to make the station look attractive, that is, with rockeries, rose bushes, lawns, etc. He continued with the measuring system, and those who averaged a rating of 4 or more for the month were invited to a party of "pap and wors". (He had no official funds to finance the parties, so he obtained sponsorships from various businessmen in town.)

Ten months after he was appointed station master, the station was on TV news. They had won the trophy for the most attractive station in the country.

> The pride generated among the workers was quite unbelievable, particularly that of the worker in charge of the garden at the front of the station. His garden always looked spick and span and the copper tap always gleamed brightly.
>
> One day a passenger used the tap and left it running, causing quite a mess. The gardener was so infuriated that he "arrested" the man and brought him before the station master.

The attractiveness of the grounds was not the only aspect that was measured. Among other things, the station master measured the length of time that parcels which arrived by rail were kept in storage at the station before being delivered in town.

It is anybody's guess what the average storage time is at most South African stations, but at this station it is seven hours. Those goods sheds always seem to be empty and the gang bosses were very proud to show me the graphs on the notice-board indicating their good performance. (No wonder the businessmen in town are willing to sponsor a party when they get that kind of service.)

Even assembly line work can be measured

I have had several managers say to me that in the situations that I quote as examples it is easy to measure the performance of workers, but that in their situation it is not possible. That may be true in some cases, but I suspect that in the majority of cases it is just an excuse not to do any measuring.

If there is one situation that I have always thought difficult to measure, it is the task of the assembly line worker. Yet in the large vehicle manufacturing plant at Rosslyn the principle of measurement is applied very successfully.

In the spot welding section, for example, every welder has to weld the same spots on each of about 25 vehicle bodies that come past his welding station. At the end of each day the foreman takes one of those vehicles at random and inspects every weld. When no faults are found, a blue spot is put next to the welder's name on a chart that is pinned on the wall at his work station. If a fault is found, it is pointed out to the worker and a red spot appears on his chart.

> The foreman does not scold the worker who makes a mistake, but reminds him how to do it correctly, by going over the training manual with him. When two red spots appear in a row, however, the foreman has to give an account of why the problem has not been corrected.
>
> That is a very sound management principle. A supervisor should never be held responsible for the mistakes that his subordinates make, but he must be held responsible if the mistakes are not rectified.

The shop floor manager told me how proud most of those spot welders have become, because many of them score only blue spots month after month. It is also noticeable that towards the end of the month they become extra careful, and any potential problem is immediately brought to the attention of the foreman. They don't want a red spot on their charts.

The result has been a dramatic increase in the quality of the welding, from approximately 65 per cent to over 99 per cent. After six years the high standard is still maintained. In 1989 the team that performed the best maintained a score of 99,8 per cent. The team that performed the poorest, averaged 98,7 per cent. There has also been a marked improvement in the morale of the workers, and absenteeism (also indicated on the notice-board) has dropped significantly.

Other aspects such as housekeeping are also measured. On a rotating basis every member of a work team is given the responsibility for the neatness of his team's area. The housekeeping is then measured regularly by the foreman and the rating (out of 5 points) is posted on the notice-board. Suddenly everyone is concerned about good housekeeping.

In the past all damaged parts were put on a table and the guilty party severely reprimanded. That, of course, "taught" workers to hide damaged parts. Today, each operator is measured by the number of parts damaged. An explanation as to the reason is all that is required from the operator – but those who have no damaged parts are given that recognition by means of a blue dot on their chart.

In 1983 damage costs came to approximately R7 per vehicle. In 1989 they were down to 16 c per vehicle. In 1989 the cost of rework was 5 per cent of what it had been in 1983 – and that while the rate of production had increased by 70 per cent.

Safety is another aspect that is measured regularly, with the result that the 1989 injury rate (DIFR) was only 22 per cent of what it had been in 1983.

Assembly line work must surely rate as one of the most boring jobs there can be, because the workers never do a completed task that they can identify as their own. Yet measuring their individual performance at least gives them some sense of achievement.

Motivating for training

Another example of the impact that measurement has on motivation is the system that this vehicle manufacturer uses to encourage training. At each work station, every team member's name appears on a grid on which every work activity performed at that station is also listed. Next to each worker's name (and for every task) there is an indication of whether he is able (a) to do the task, (b) to do the task in standard time and (c) to teach someone else to do the task. This grid is posted on the notice-board.

The impact has been two-fold. The workers ask to be trained in other activities because it affects their pride when the grid shows that they are capable of doing only one or two of the tasks. They are also keen to teach others to do their tasks. It is also an indication to the shop floor manager as to how well a foreman would be able to cope if any of his workers were absent. It shows him how much effort each foreman puts into training. This in turn motivates the foremen to devote a good deal of their time to training.

Conclusion

Nobody can experience a sense of achievement unless that achievement is measured. In order to measure achievement management has to agree with subordinates on the goals that they must pursue – and these goals must obviously be measurable.

Some managers claim that they do not have the time to measure the performance of all their subordinates. In most cases the real reason is that they are too busy supervising ("snoopervising") the activities of their subordinates.

It requires a major shift in emphasis to move away from checking on *activities* to measuring *end results*. Several managers who have made a concerted effort to apply the human resource theory have told me that their main problem was to change their own thinking.

10 RESPONSIBILITY FOR DECISION MAKING

What is responsibility?

Managers often confuse the word "responsibility" with the word "duty". If I say to a janitor that it is his responsibility to keep the floors clean, will that motivate him? Certainly not! I might just as well have said that it is his duty to keep the floor clean.

What kind of responsibility motivates subordinates? When they are allowed to use their own *judgment*, when they have the right to make a *decision* themselves, when they have the authority to use their own *discretion* in dealing with a problem.

> A farmer had a small workshop where he employed one "mechanic", Elias, although he did most of the work himself. He frequently blamed Elias for tools that were missing (especially the No. 13 spanner), although he realised that the tractor drivers were just as much to blame.
>
> On his return from my management seminar he did two things. He asked Elias to devise a system for keeping control of the spanners and he told him that from now on he would have to do all the repairs himself and call the farmer only when he was stuck.
>
> A few days later the farmer came to fetch a pair of pliers from the workshop and was told by Elias that he was "number one" and that a little disc with "1" on it would be hung in the place where the pliers were kept.
>
> He had allocated a number to everyone on the farm who made use of tools, and the result was that in the next six months no tools were lost.
>
> Even more significant was the fact that Elias did an extremely good job in keeping the vehicles repaired. The farmer was amazed to discover how good a mechanic Elias really was. He became a very valuable and a very motivated employee because he was al-

> lowed to use his own judgment, while the farmer had time to become a manager.

A sense of responsibility is not a personality trait. So often managers believe that a subordinate's sense of responsibility (or lack of it) is determined by the way he has been brought up by his parents. This may have had some influence, but the factor that really determines whether a person has a sense of responsibility or not, is simply how much responsibility he has been *given*.

Why does responsibility motivate?

Take the typical example of a subordinate facing a particular problem in the work situation. He goes to his manager and not only tells him what the problem is but also offers a solution. If the boss's response is: "No, that's not the answer. What you must do is . . . " the subordinate will then do what the boss has told him to do, but he has no real commitment to making it work. Why should he? It was not his solution. In fact, he may even feel resentful that his proposal was rejected and deliberately make the boss's plan fail.

How different the response would have been if the boss had said: "Are you sure that will work? All right, let's try it." Immediately the subordinate would have had an emotional investment in that solution. He will do everything in his power to make it work because it was *his* solution.

> Obviously when a subordinate proposes a completely wrong solution, the manager must help him by asking questions to direct his thinking, not telling him what the "right" solution is.
>
> Telling him he is wrong will only have the effect of switching him off in the future and letting the boss do the thinking – and the manager is the poorer for it.

Who is responsible?

Responsibility can never be conveyed to workers by *telling* them that they are responsible. That means nothing. The only person who is responsible is the one who makes the decisions. A bank manager may, for example, give the responsibility for approving credit loans to his loans officer (within certain parameters), but if the loans officer one day turns down an application for credit and the client appeals directly to the bank manager, the issue of responsibility is at stake. The moment the bank manager overrides the decision of the loans officer he has taken back the responsibility; only one person can be responsible for any given decision.

In fact, responsibility has not been given to a subordinate until the manager is willing to put himself under the authority of the subordinate on that particular area of responsibility.

A farmer near Warmbaths started measuring the performance of his drivers on the running costs of their tractors. He painted each driver's name on the bonnet of his tractor, and their pride was obvious for all to see. Not only was there a significant drop in the running costs, but three-year old tractors looked almost brand new – even the tyres were polished on Saturday afternoons.

One weekend the farmer told one of the drivers that he wanted to use his tractor for a particular task. "Sorry, Boss, you don't drive my tractor. I'll do it for you," was the response.

The farmer had to accept the driver's "authority" because a driver cannot be held responsible for the condition of his vehicle unless he has the authority to decide who may drive it – and even the boss is subject to that authority.

Either the driver is responsible for his vehicle, or the manager is – they cannot both be.

This point is brought home quite forcibly by Goddard (1986:82), who describes some of the essential ingredients for implementing a successful "Just in time" programme. The only way companies could increase the quality of their products was by putting the responsibility for quality on the shoulders of the operators themselves. This, however, meant that every operator had the right to stop the entire production line in order to solve a quality problem. Some production managers had a hard time subjecting themselves to this "authority", yet the results overwhelmingly justified the means.

Green areas in a motorcar plant

One of the reasons for the amazing successes of the car manufacturing plant referred to in chapter 9, is a concept that they have termed "green areas" (to emphasise the need for fresh ideas). At each of the more than two hundred work stations in the plant an area has been set aside with a table and benches. During the first ten minutes of every day the foreman sits at the table with his subordinates and they discuss the previous day's results as well as any work problems facing them that day.

These sessions started out as an exercise in one-way communication, but soon developed into problem-solving sessions. Foremen were taught how to encourage the workers to come up with the solutions themselves – and it immediately created a strong sense of commitment and team spirit among the workers.

Since these "green areas" were implemented, they have not had a single strike owing to "poor labour practices" – because workers are beginning to identify themselves with the company.

> Later a crudely painted sign appeared high in the factory rafters: "We are . . . (name of company) and we are proud of it."
> That's the kind of employee morale all managers would love to have in their company.

Motivating roads foremen

People are very sceptical when I ask them if they think it is possible to motivate the supervisor who sits in the yellow truck with his newspaper and coffee flask while the road workers are busy. We often criticise him, but he operates like this because of the way he is managed.

In most provinces a roads superintendent is put in charge of a certain geographical area. He has inspectors travelling throughout the area to determine what work needs to be done. Each day the assistant roads foreman (the chap in the yellow truck) is told what to do and where. What choice does he have? He can only collect his workers and watch them at work (while the public criticise him for "doing nothing").

In one of our provinces the situation has now changed. Each assistant roads foreman (ARF) has been given a section of roads to be *his* responsibility alone. Instead of being told what needs to be done, the ARF now decides *himself* what the priorities are in his area. He then submits a weekly work plan and at the end of the week submits a detailed report of what has been done. (Delegating responsibility does not imply abdication. The manager still has to exercise sound management control.) At the end of the month the quality of the roads in his area is inspected and evaluated by the roads superintendent.

The result has been a tremendous upsurge in motivation and commitment on the part of the ARFs. They are now beginning to speak of "my roads" and several of them have requested training on how they can motivate *their* workers.

The methods vary; the principles are the same. Whenever workers are allowed to use their own judgment in the execution of their tasks, the work itself becomes meaningful to them, a source of pride.

"Defendable territory"

One of the key facets of motivation is for work to be allocated in such a way that workers can develop a sense of identity with the task as a whole. This is not always easy, especially when expensive machinery is involved. In many cases, however, managers have never even thought of rearranging the design of the tasks in their unit.

One of the successful human resource managers that I have had the pleasure of working with stressed how important it was for every one of his subordinates to have an area that he could identify with as his responsibility. He coined the phrase "defendable territory" that the worker could call his own.

> At a large manufacturing company the work of the cost controllers was designed very much along the lines of an assembly line. A large number of products was involved and each clerk had to calculate certain aspects of each product's costs. The result of this kind of work allocation was that none of them ever did a "completed job".
>
> The head of the department then reallocated the work in such a way that each cost controller had full responsibility for the entire costing of specific products.
>
> The result was that, with time, each controller started to build

up his own record files on specific products. Because they had the "whole picture" they could liaise directly with the technical departments to question certain aspects or clarify something that they did not understand. They were even able to liaise with some of their major clients.

Each cost controller had a "defendable territory" and it was not long before they were talking of "my products". The level of commitment became so high that from an original staff of seventeen cost controllers, the job is now being handled by eight.

The department head also gave them gradually more and more opportunities to use their own judgment. He allowed them, for example, to plan the annual stocktaking themselves. They determined the exact dates, the format of the control sheet, the detailed procedures, as well as the norms for determining the value of the stock items. The result? Stocktaking became enjoyable.

"Blankets must be left at home"

The station master referred to in the previous chapter ascribes his success to the fact that every Friday he has six meetings with his entire staff (25 employees per meeting). There he shares with them management information. Even the porters and the groundsmen are put in the picture as to how the station is doing income-wise, cost-wise, etc. He makes use of graphs and bar charts, and then he spends the rest of the meeting asking them for their ideas on how to make the station even more effective.

I asked one of the workers why they were working so hard, compared with previous years. His answer said it all: "Morena, you cannot bring your blanket to work. You have to leave your blanket at home, because here you have to be wide awake."

That was his way of saying that they were now required to think.

The result of this motivating action (besides winning the trophy for the most beautiful station in the country) was that in his first year the station master had 18 absentee days, compared with 553 days the year before. He had to deal with only 10 disciplinary cases that year, compared with 314 the previous year; and he was 58 per cent below his expense budget, representing a saving of more than R300 000.

No wonder the general manager sent him a ticket for taking his family to Cape Town on the Blue Train, spending a few days in a hotel (including pocket money) and coming back by SAA!

Countering the union

One day the station master received a call from the local postmaster informing him that the following Monday the postal workers and railway workers were going to strike in sympathy with the strikes taking place on the Reef at that time.

The postal workers stayed away, but every railway worker was at work that Monday morning. The reason is very important to understand. Workers always strike *against* something or someone. When they are involved in the decision-making process, however, it becomes very difficult to identify who they are against, because the distinction between labour and management is no longer clearly demarcated.

> A trade union can operate only on the basis of management versus labour. It's *us* against *them*. This is possible only if there is a clear dividing line between management and labour, and in most organisations such a line is clearly distinguishable.
>
> What is that line? It is the *decision-making* line. The people above the line (the managers) make the decisions, while people below the line (the workers) carry them out.
>
> Many companies have tried to minimise the power of the unions by providing their employees with everything the union might agitate for. They make sure that their wages are above the industry average, that they have a sound grievance procedure, that as far as possible racial discrimination is eliminated, etc.
>
> Yet such measures have not been very successful in reducing labour conflict, because it does not affect the decision-making line.
>
> A large agricultural organisation in the Transvaal, however, has been practising the human resource theory for some years. They

have approximately 1 500 workers, yet theirs is the only company in the group which has not been unionised – and it is not for want of trying on the part of the union. It's just that the workers themselves see no need for a union.

Albert Koopman had the same experience. After the workers at Cashbuild became involved in decision making the union membership among the employees became negligible.

Who is responsible for problem solving?

Workers often accept their work situation as a given fact over which they have little control, because managers have conditioned them to think that way. ("I'm responsible for the thinking, you're responsible for the doing.") The result is that they simply switch off.

One of the key factors that increases a manager's effectiveness is his ability to develop the thinking abilities of his subordinates. This is done not only by giving them the responsibility for making the ongoing decisions in their work, but also by letting them solve the problems that arise in their work situation. There is abundant evidence that when workers are given the responsibility for solving their own work problems, they not only come up with good ideas, but they are totally committed to making the solution work.

At a large corporation in Natal six typists (or rather, word processing operators) were extremely frustrated. Over a long period of time their work had been piling up to such an extent that they were two weeks behind, with very little prospect of catching up. Some of them even claimed that the pressure at work was also creating tension at home.

The department head encouraged them to tackle the problem themselves, so they started off by identifying all the problem areas:
☐ Poor handwriting by the authors
☐ Constant retyping of authors' corrections
☐ Redoing the work of other typists who had not followed the correct procedures

After lengthy discussions and deliberations, they drew up a form letter whereby a draft was returned to the author if it didn't meet certain standards. (They pointed out that they were trying to improve their service, and invited anybody who was unhappy to come and discuss it. Nobody complained.)

They also decided that no document would be amended more than four times and they drew up a manual to standardise typing procedures throughout the company.

The result was that within a matter of months their average backlog was one day, and they seldom exceeded the goal of two days that they had set for themselves. What's more, there were only four operators left in the department, and they were very proud of their achievement.

One of the most effective ways of encouraging workers to use their creativity for solving problems is to introduce *quality circles*. This is a formalised system whereby groups of workers (preferably from the same department but sometimes from different departments) meet regularly to tackle a specific problem that has been identified by the group members themselves. The group is led by a team leader who has usually had some skills training on how to lead such discussion groups. The solutions they wish to implement are then presented to management for approval.

Numerous books have been written on the implementation and functioning of such groups (e.g. Hutchins 1985), but by far the most important prerequisite for success is support from management. Support for the concept is, however, not enough; support in implementing the solutions must also be given.

Creating "thinking workers"

Some years ago a director of one of our large motor vehicle manufacturing companies near Durban returned from Japan inspired with the objective of "creating thinking workers" and two senior managers were singled out to achieve this goal. They started off slowly with a specialist group of workers who were assigned to a specific production line to identify problems and then make recommendations on how to solve them.

This group initially identified the need for additional facilities that would cost R96 000 to implement. Their proposal met with a fair amount of resistance, but they were able to convince management that they could recoup that amount within two years. As it turned out, they recouped it within seven months.

Although it started with a success story, it took several years for the concept to take hold within the organisation, since it required intensive training. However, over a period of time both specialist groups and quality circles increased in number. After five years they had ninety active quality circles.

As the groups increased, so the number of successes increased. Whenever a group came up with some improvement, they were invited to make a presentation to the directors and plant management. In 1984 they made a total of 13 such presentations, while in 1988 there were 152 presentations.

The success stories were also written up in the company journal with accompanying photographs. Not only was this an important source of recognition, it also encouraged others to get in on the act.

However, the success rate was not 100 per cent. There were cases where the implementation of quality circles failed. There were several main reasons for this:
- ☐ Groups were pressurised by management to start a quality circle because it was "the in thing".
- ☐ Management tended to identify the problem, rather than the group itself. Usually these problems were so difficult that the group became disheartened and gave up.
- ☐ After a group presented an acceptable solution, it was not implemented. The group disbanded.

"Customer" satisfaction

The next phase in their pursuit of "creating thinking workers" came when they embarked on a quality programme based on the philosophy that each worker on the assembly line is the "customer" of the preceding worker and therefore entitled to receive fault-free work.

It all started with a black communications officer from the training department who would go into an area where there was a recurring quality problem. He would then trace the source of the problem, recommend a solution and monitor it for two weeks, until the problem was solved.

Nobody was ever reprimanded (a typical South African solution), and the fact that it was a black man explaining to the "problem" operator what difficulties were being experienced down the line made it more acceptable.

Eventually over five hundred supervisors were trained in the skill of tracing a quality problem and dealing with it at its source. Quality was no longer the responsibility of the quality control department. It was now the workers themselves who were responsible for the quality of the work produced in their unit.

Getting operators to think

At this stage management realised that the bulk of the workforce was still not actively involved. To participate in most of the specialist groups required a certain level of education that the majority of the workers did not have, and not everyone wanted to participate in a quality circle.

A survey was undertaken to determine what the workers wanted (besides wages, benefits, facilities, etc.). The survey highlighted three needs, namely *respect, limited authority* and *someone to listen*. (This was just another way of saying that they wanted a sense of achievement, responsibility and recognition.)

To satisfy these needs a programme was initiated to involve and teach workers at the lowest levels how to make improvements. Operators were invited to attend training courses on a Saturday morning. This was a five hour course presented in Zulu and it focused on giving the trainees as many practical examples as possible – often with the use of videos – of all the aspects of their work that could be improved. On each course the trainers also involved an "old hand" to tell some of the success stories of the past and to take the participants to his work area to show them some of the improvements that had been brought about.

Management started with operators from areas where there was a good likelihood of success (e.g. trainees who had supervisors who were very supportive of the programme). In selling the idea to workers to start thinking, management avoided the word *productivity*. Such a word does not exist in Zulu and it often has a negative connotation for the worker. It gives the impression he *must* work harder. In this company management promoted the idea of "improving the quality of work life". That is why workers who have made a presentation to management are given a little badge with "I work smarter, not harder" on it.

One of the aids to get operators thinking creatively was a "waste" questionnaire to focus on ways to eliminate unnecessary work. This checklist directs thinking to specific problem areas by asking questions like: "Do you have to walk around a fixture, a table, or a rack to get to your components?" The questionnaire is available in English and in Zulu, and asks 65 such questions that have to be answered "Yes", "No", or "?".

> One of the assembly line workers came up with an idea to stack his components in a specially designed rack that would mean that he would not have to walk so far to get the parts that he had to fit onto the vehicle.
>
> After his idea was implemented, it was calculated that he actually walked 2,05 km less each day.
>
> It turned out that he had had this idea for almost a year before doing anything about it. When he was asked why he had not suggested it earlier, his response was: "But I'm only an operator."
>
> It just brought home again to management the fact that so many workers are conditioned not to think.

Just as with the quality circles, success stories were given recognition by means of presentations to management as well as pictures in the company magazine. In making these presentations the workers are assisted by a black trainer who sketches the improvement on an overhead transparency. Every Friday a few hours are set aside for such presentations. Although they are attended by various managers from the factory, they are conducted entirely by the workers themselves. It is their show.

There were 130 presentations in 1986, 584 in 1987, 1 048 in 1988, and management expected well over a thousand in 1989. If one considers that each presentation means a new idea for improvement, the implications are staggering. No wonder some of the plant managers are no longer surprised at the tremendous creativity displayed by the workers.

> One would have expected the ideas to run dry after some time, but they just seem to increase with the years.

> Several magazine articles have been written about the remarkable success that this company has achieved in utilising the creativity of their workers. The savings don't run into thousands, they run into millions. They have truly succeeded in "creating thinking workers".

Above all, these programmes have contributed significantly to the labour relations climate in the company. Strikes have not been eliminated totally, but they occur less frequently and are usually restricted to a specific section in the plant.

Conclusion

Whether a company makes use of quality circles, has project teams for tackling specific problems, implements "Just in time" programmes or just holds informal problem-solving discussions as and when a problem arises, it all boils down to the same basic principles:
- ☐ Workers have a great deal of untapped potential.
- ☐ One of management's most important tasks is to harness that potential.
- ☐ When workers are involved in problem-solving it stimulates the kind of commitment that every manager is looking for from his subordinates.

11 RECOGNITION OF ACHIEVEMENT

Everybody wants to know

Recognition is probably one of the most powerful motivational tools available to a manager because every person has a basic need to know what the boss thinks of him.

> The story is told of a gardener called Amos who went to a public call box and phoned his employer without identifying himself.
> "Good day, Sir, do you have a gardener?" he asked.
> "Yes, thank you very much. I have a gardener," said the employer.
> "Is he very good? Can you leave him to work on his own?" asked Amos.
> "Yes, he's an excellent worker, I don't need anybody else, thank you," came the rather curt reply.
> "Sir, does he wash and polish your car every week?" continued Amos.
> "Yesss, my car is always shining!" replied the employer impatiently.
> "Sir, can you use him as a waiter when you have guests?" persisted Amos.
> By this time the employer was almost shouting: "*Yes!* He can do everything! Who's speaking?"
> "Boss, this is Amos. I just wanted to know if you're still satisfied."

Loving in secret

What do subordinates do when they do not receive any feedback from their managers? If the manager is lucky, his subordinates will do nothing. But there is a good likelihood that they will start causing trouble. The Bible

(Proverbs 27:5) says: "An open rebuke is better than secret love." What is secret love? It's a case of having a subordinate who is performing well but who is never complimented. You just "love him in secret".

Every now and then I hear of a real troublemaker in the firm being promoted to supervisor – and in each case he has turned out to be a very successful manager. Why? A troublemaker is usually someone who has leadership and initiative, but is crying out for some recognition. When he is promoted to a position of leadership, all his abilities are harnessed into a productive channel.

I once counselled a young man of 21 who was really rebellious. When I asked him about it, he said: "I wasn't very good at schoolwork, and I didn't achieve much on the sportsfield, but those teachers will always remember me." Rebellion was his way of becoming "somebody".

> I was consulted by the owners of a small factory in Johannesburg which had just been unionised. There had always been a good relationship between management and the work force of about forty workers, but since they had been unionised the atmosphere was one of hostility and aggression. What upset management the most was that their best worker had organised the union.
>
> In discussions it became clear that, although she was their best worker, they had very seldom given her that recognition. They had "loved her in secret".
>
> Once she was appointed as shop steward, she wielded a tremendous amount of influence and management had constantly to consult her on labour matters.
>
> She was now "somebody", but to management's detriment, and they only had themselves to blame.

How do you know you're doing a good job?

I am sometimes asked to do a survey of the management climate in an organisation. I usually do this by holding interviews. One of the questions I always ask employees is: "How do you know that you are doing a good job?" I get all kinds of answers, but the most frequent one is: "Well, nobody has ever told me I'm doing a bad job. I assume that my boss is satisfied with my work." How sad it is that the only way that some people know whether the boss is satisfied is from the lack of negative comment.

In one company, however, two employees (in two separate interviews) showed me a letter of congratulations.

> *Dear Joe*
> *I have just been informed of your achievement on your last project. Congratulations! Keep up the good work. We need people like you in our company.*
> *Signed: Managing Director*

One of those letters was four months old, but the worker still carried it in his pocket. It was obvious how much it meant to him. Albert Koopman (1987:220) frequently sent a note of congratulations whenever he heard of any staff member doing a particularly outstanding job. (He also made a point of sending a note when he was not satisfied – but that aspect is dealt with in chapter 16.)

A training manager in the Northern Transvaal told me that he had been a teacher for eighteen years. In that time he "never" received any recognition. The last straw was when he had coached a rugby team over a period of two years. They went on tour through Natal during the school holidays and won every match. The headmaster of the school, who was on holiday in Durban at the time, came to watch the final match, and when the press took a photograph of this unbeaten team, guess who posed with the team? The headmaster. What bothered this teacher the most, however, was that the headmaster did not give him a single word of praise, nor did he point out to the press that it was the coach who deserved the credit.

That was the final blow. He resigned and took up a position as training manager. After three months with his new firm, he presented his first training course. A favourable report on the course ended up on the general manager's desk and came back with two words written on top: "Well done!" and the signature of the GM.

He told me that when he saw those two words it was as if a new world had opened up for him. He suddenly had the feeling that there was a future for him with this organisation.

You have the subordinates you deserve

What effect does it have on a person when he is given an honest compliment?

> The word "honest" is the key. Subordinates are very quick to sense any form of flattery or insincerity on the part of a manager – that would cause more harm than saying nothing.

A sincere compliment has the effect of creating a very strong desire on the part of the recipient to maintain the standard, if not improve on it. If a truck driver is congratulated on how low the running costs of his vehicle are, it would be very difficult for him to adopt a careless attitude towards his truck. Criticism, on the other hand, has the effect of reinforcing the negative behaviour.

> During a marriage counselling session a husband was telling me of all the things his wife did wrong. He listed them one by one. Amongst others, he told me what "lousy food" he was given each evening.
>
> I turned to his wife who was sitting next to him, and asked her to tell me about this "lousy food". She replied quite sharply: "He's always telling me what a poor cook I am. Why should I bother?"
>
> She had become exactly what he said she was, and it again highlighted the fact that every person has the marriage partner he or she deserves. If you have a terrific partner, it's probably because you've built them up that way. If you're married to a miserable person, it's probably because you have broken them down so much with your criticism.

I believe that every manager has the subordinates he deserves. Some managers have subordinates who are totally committed to their work – and they make the manager look good. Other managers have subordinates who only give them ulcers and grey hairs. It depends on the extent to which they have built their subordinates up or broken them down.

Reluctance to praise others

Despite the obvious impact that a sincere compliment has on a subordinate, managers seem very reluctant to express their praise. We live in a society where little is said if things go well, but we are quick to raise our voices when things go wrong.

> At one seminar a man told me that the previous evening he had sat down to dinner in his home, but had pushed his pudding away because he didn't like it.
> His wife blew her top. "You are never satisfied with the food that I prepare. You never have anything good to say about my food. You always criticise my cooking."
> "That's not true," he replied, "last night I said nothing."

Why are managers so reluctant to praise their subordinates when they have done a good job? Perhaps they are afraid that the subordinates will expect something more tangible in the form of a raise or even a promotion. It is true that good performance should be rewarded with some form of material recognition when it comes to salary reviews, but this is certainly not expected during the course of the year.

The fear that a subordinate will ask for some kind of a handout if he is praised is ungrounded. In fact the very opposite may be true. In many cases employees who ask the manager for a raise or a promotion are simply asking for some kind of recognition. It's their way of finding out "if the boss is still satisfied".

Another reason why some managers are so reluctant to praise their subordinates may be the way they were brought up. If a person seldom received praise as a child, it is very likely that he will not give praise to those around him.

> A farmer told me that he had been brought up in a home where his father never complimented him. He remembers the day when he was top of his science class with 85 per cent and his father made him feel bad because he didn't get 90 per cent. The result was that he found it difficult to compliment his wife or children, let alone his workers.

> On returning from my seminar, he went to see how his workers had progressed with the building of a dam wall. To his surprise they were doing an outstanding job and he suddenly became aware that he needed to praise them – but he couldn't say it. The words seemed to stick in his throat.
>
> Finally he clapped his hands in appreciation, put his thumb up, and walked away embarrassed. However, when he looked back, he saw smiling faces and this loosened something inside of him.
>
> Today he is not only a successful human resource manager; his family have blossomed in every respect as they have responded to his positive feedback.

We do not have to remain the victims of our past experiences. While they undoubtedly affect our behaviour, there is nothing preventing us from changing – except our own will. Time and again managers have said to me that the problem does not lie with their subordinates, it lies with themselves. Whenever they apply the human resource principles, their subordinates respond positively – their main problem is disciplining themselves to behave differently.

Numerous forms of recognition

There are numerous ways in which managers can give recognition to their subordinates. The most obvious one is a sincere compliment to the person concerned. This need not be in a formal setting – that can be done once a year when the manager conducts a performance appraisal interview with the subordinate. Recognition can be given frequently and need be nothing more than giving your subordinate a thumbs-up sign, or saying: "The figures this month look very good."

> A senior manager of a large corporation told me during a management meeting that he did not have the time to tell his subordinates each month that they were doing a good job. He had seven immediate subordinates.
>
> I told him that if he was too busy to give that kind of feedback to seven people once a month, he was too busy.

> Some of his subordinates sitting in front of him kept dead still, but a few of his subordinates sitting behind him nodded their heads vigorously in agreement.
> He was too busy to be a good manager.

Other means of giving employees positive feedback is to write them a letter of appreciation when they have done a particularly outstanding job. This is the kind of thing a man can take home to his family. Photographs in the company journal are another means of recognising the contribution of individuals.

> The factory manager at a large motor car manufacturing plant was approached by one of the operators on the shop floor, who told him that a photograph of his team had appeared in the company magazine because of the good results they had achieved.
> The factory manager wasn't sure what the operator was getting at until he showed him the photograph and said: "Sir, do you see that man on the left of the picture? I was standing next to him." He had been cut out of the picture.
> It was only then that the factory manager realised how important that photograph had been for the operator and he took steps to ensure that such an oversight did not occur again.

Other means of recognition include special awards (ranging from a certificate of merit to a gold watch), overseas trips, a weekend at a holiday resort, etc.

Avoid competitions

One kind of recognition that is suspect is the "Worker of the Month" award. This generates competition among employees who have to work together, and competitions generally do more to demotivate people than to motivate them.

A manager instituted a "Driver of the Month" competition among his five truck drivers. The first month everybody tried hard but, of course, only one driver won. The second month another driver won, and the third month the first driver won again.

After that the others stopped trying, with the excuse that they weren't really interested. This was to save face, because everybody knows that it is better not to try than to try and then fail.

To stimulate the other drivers to try again, the manager let some of them "win", even though their performance was not particularly good. Now he was being dishonest. He also demotivated the two who were genuinely making an effort.

It would have been far more effective to give an award to every driver who achieved his goal as far as running costs were concerned. They would then have been competing against themselves and not against each other.

He could have had five winners each month.

Some companies try to "motivate" their salesmen by offering a round-the-world trip as first prize to the person who achieves the highest sales. I think a company like that is wasting its money. How many salesmen really work to win that prize? Two or three at the most. Since there can only be one winner, only one salesman is likely to be motivated afterwards.

A far better investment of that prize money would be if every salesman who exceeded his own target by 30 per cent (or whatever) were given a weekend for two at a luxury hotel. For the same expense the company could give recognition (and subsequent motivation) to at least twenty of their salesmen.

Publishing performance results

In the light of the negative consequences of competition, the question arises whether individual performance results should be made known. There is no clear-cut answer to this. It depends very much on how management uses the figures. If the published figures are used to stimulate competition, the effect may be very negative, particularly among employees who have to work together. There have been numerous cases of good performers being sabotaged by their fellow workers because they make them look bad.

> A sugar cane farmer in Natal wrote on a big board how much cane each cutter had cut and stacked. After the third day, the stacks of the better performers were knocked over.

On the other hand, if management's policy is to encourage individuals or departments to compete against themselves, and "winners" are given recognition, the publication of performance figures will not have a serious detrimental effect. It will serve as a boost for those people who are the top achievers, while not necessarily letting the less successful performers feel that they are losers.

The important thing for management is to create as many "winners" and as few "losers" as possible in the company.

Conclusion

I am convinced that recognition is probably the most powerful motivator available to a manager. At the same time it is the most neglected one. Perhaps the main reason is the fact that management does not always know what results their subordinates have achieved.

This brings us back to the importance of measurement (see chapter 9). When subordinates are measured in terms of the end results that they have achieved, feedback and recognition follow almost automatically.

Part 4
Managing people

12 THE TASK OF THE MANAGER

Summary

The task of a manager involves a great deal more than just managing subordinates. A manager has to manage machinery, materials, money, etc. depending on the nature of his function. However, the focus of this book is the issue of managing the most important resource of all, namely people. Even then issues such as recruitment and selection, wage and salary administration, performance appraisal, labour relations, training programmes, etc. fall beyond the scope of this book. I have chosen to focus on the effective utilisation of subordinates.

The task of the manager when it comes to utilising subordinates is twofold:
- [ ] To *treat* his subordinates in such a way that there is no *cause* for complaint or dissatisfaction.
- [ ] To *motivate* his subordinates in such a way that their abilities will be *utilised* to the full.

What is a manager responsible for?

If those are the two basic tasks of a manager as far as managing people is concerned, who is responsible for sales in a company? The sales manager or the sales representatives? Many of us would have no hesitation in arguing that the sales manager is responsible, but is that his real task?

> Let's take the example of a sales manager who has ten representatives working under him. The sales team's target was R10 m and at the end of the year the sales figure stood at R10,5 m. How would you rate the sales manager? Most of us would agree that he was successful.
> Would you still say that he was successful, if you discovered that

99

he sold R8 m himself and each of his reps sold R250 000? No! Most of us would agree that he is a successful salesman – not a successful manager.

This sales manager believes that he is responsible for the sales, and that his subordinates are just there to help him. He failed as a manager because he did not carry out his most important task – that of motivating his salesmen.

If the sales figure at the end of the year had been R9 m, who would have been held accountable? The sales manager, of course. But what would he have been accountable for? For not bringing in enough sales, or for not motivating his representatives sufficiently?

If his superior reprimands him for not bringing in sufficient sales, the sales manager will rush out and start selling. If he is reprimanded for not motivating his subordinates enough, he will focus on improving their performance.

We have to be very clear on what the task of a manager really is.

If a manager is to be successful, he must not only know what the expectations of his subordinates are, but also take active steps to meet those expectations. I am convinced that there are universal expectations that apply to the majority of employees at all levels in the organisation. What are those expectations?

Good treatment

In chapter 7 I discussed some of the expectations that employees have when it comes to good *treatment*:
- "Provide me with favourable working conditions."
- "Maintain a pleasant relationship with me."
- "Deal with me fairly."

I cannot sufficiently stress the importance of this issue. If these three expectations are not met adequately, most attempts at motivating subordinates will fail.

When workers are highly motivated, they will be more willing to accept unfavourable conditions or poor treatment than when their

> jobs are boring – but there is a limit to what an employee is prepared to endure.

In the definition of the manager's task I stressed the word *cause* because, like the poor, the gripers and the moaners will always be with us. It would be absurd for management to try to please everybody all the time. Such people need to be ignored or, if their job performance is not up to standard, replaced.

Management must, however, be quite sure that there isn't a genuine *reason* for dissatisfaction, and the area that they need to be particularly sensitive to is the question of *perceived unfairness*, especially when it comes to money.

> A technician at a manufacturing plant complained bitterly to me that the company had just appointed another technician, with less experience, at a higher salary than he was getting.
>
> Management might have been "forced" to offer the newcomer the higher wage in order to attract him to the company, but in the process they will probably lose another good technician – achieving nothing in the exchange except a higher wage bill.

Keeping an ear to the ground

How does management determine whether there are major sources of discontent in the organisation? All too often managers higher up in the company are totally out of touch with what is going on at the lower levels. Many of them rely on the reports they receive from their immediate subordinates, who, of course, will only tell the boss what he wants to hear. To counteract this problem I strongly recommend MBWA (management by walking around). This implies that a manager must take the time to talk to employees at all levels in his division or department.

How much time a manager should spend on "the shop floor" is a controversial topic. Some authors recommend that managers should spend a great deal of time talking to employees two or three levels below them, others say that managers should not talk to workers down the line since this would be undermining the authority of the workers' immediate supervisor.

Both points of view are correct. It all depends on what the manager does on his walkabouts. If he gives instructions to workers or reprimands them in any way (i.e. acts from a position of authority), the effects over the long term will be disastrous. The immediate supervisor would be completely hamstrung in his management efforts and the morale in his unit would soon take a nose dive.

If, on the other hand, the manager uses his walkabouts to take an interest in the individual workers, ask questions, give compliments, even have the occasional social chat to an operator, he will not only boost morale but also ensure that he keeps his ear to the ground for any potential problem area.

> That does not mean the manager must ignore a situation that is obviously wrong; he must just not take action on his own to correct it. He should report it to the supervisor in the spirit of: "I'm here to help you."

The importance of MBWA, especially by top management, cannot be overemphasised. Management must be visible, but the workers should see management as a source of support rather than a source of interference. I was told of a company where the only time the workers ever saw the managing director was when he appeared on television. Employees need to know that management genuinely cares about the quality of their work life.

> The personnel manager of a large timber company told me that the major reason for resignations in his company is the fact that workers feel "lonely".
> Senior managers very seldom take the trouble to engage in conversation with foresters at the lower levels or even bother to ask them how things are going or if they are having any problems.
> Top managers must be visible.

To augment the information that a manager picks up on his walkabouts, the manpower department (or a professional consultant) can conduct formal attitude surveys on a regular basis to monitor the morale in the organisation. These surveys are often very helpful, especially if the results are fed back to the departments concerned and used as a basis for open discussions between managers and subordinates. The benefits would be even greater if top management were to insist on a report from middle managers on the action they are going to take to correct any negative aspect highlighted by the survey.

Motivation

What do subordinates expect from their manager when it comes to motivation? John Humble (1969:16) suggests that all subordinates have five basic expectations that will motivate them to fully utilise their abilities.
- "Agree with me on the results I must achieve."
- "Give me the opportunity to prove myself."
- "Let me know how I am doing – whether it's good or bad."
- "Give me help when I need it, or when I'm performing poorly."
- "Give me recognition for my contribution by rewarding me accordingly."

Most employees, particularly those at the lower levels in the organisation, will not be able to express their expectations in exactly those terms, but when a manager meets these five expectations, the results are very impressive.

> In South Africa it is generally agreed that the least developed employees, in terms of education and training, are farm workers. Yet there are scores of farmers across the country who have had tremendous success in motivating their workers when they started meeting these expectations.
>
> Many of these cases have been described in my book *Motivating your farm labourer* and it is quite common to hear farmers saying: "I can't believe how motivated my workers have become." Even farm labourers have these basic expectations.

Agree with me on the results I must achieve

This expectation is met when a manager sets objectives with the subordinate. They do not talk about the activities or tasks that the subordinate has to carry out, but rather about the *results* he has to achieve, thereby implying that the *method* is left to the discretion of the subordinate.

I don't like job descriptions. Drawing them up may be necessary, especially for use in job evaluation, but they tend to focus on what the job incumbent must *do* rather than on what he must *achieve*.

Give me the opportunity to prove myself

This is the common plea of subordinates throughout commerce and industry: "I wish the boss would leave me alone so I could get on with my work." Very few workers who have been given specific responsibility want their managers to leave them alone so that they can loaf. They want to be left alone so that they can show the boss what they are capable of doing. They don't want him looking over their shoulders.

> In my final year of high school I realised that I was battling to study because my mother was always telling me to do so.
> I pleaded with her to leave me alone and let me work out my own study programme – and she did.
> The result was that for the first (and last) time I could say that my school marks were *my* achievement. I fared much better at university because I was left to get on with my studies on my own.

Deep inside every person there is a need to be successful at what he is doing, to be proud of what he has accomplished. Managers who are continually telling their subordinates what to do are depriving them of the opportunity to fulfil this basic need.

There are two ways in which managers can satisfy this need: by *delegating responsibility* and by involving their subordinates in *decision making* and *problem solving*. In the first situation the subordinates are given the authority to deal with the problem themselves; in the second situation they participate actively in discussions with the manager to solve a particular problem.

Let me know how I am doing – whether it's good or bad

To be able to give subordinates feedback on their performance a manager must institute effective *management controls*. Many managers have told me that they implemented the human resource theory, but found that after some time the initial impact faded and they went back to their old ways of managing. In almost all these cases they had not instituted a formal system of control whereby the performance of their subordinates was measured and recorded in terms of the *end results*. If managers are serious about motivating their subordinates, they will have to adjust the management systems in the company accordingly.

> One of the most disappointing experiences I have had as a management consultant was with a large building society.
>
> I had spent three days at a conference of senior and branch managers negotiating the objectives and decision-making authority of the branch managers, as well as agreeing on the control measures that would be used to monitor their performance.
>
> The branch managers expressed great excitement at the fact that at last they knew what was expected of them and which decisions they were allowed to make on their own.
>
> Two weeks later a directive came from head office instructing them to obtain prior approval from senior management before taking any decisions on their own.
>
> The organisation's "control system" was still based on the traditional theory and it completely negated the motivating impact of the conference.

Give me help when I need it, or when I'm performing poorly

If the control system highlights the fact that a particular subordinate is not achieving the desired results, what does he expect from his manager? Certainly not a reprimand. That seldom accomplishes anything. It only makes him feel more like a failure. No, he expects help in order to become successful at his job.

I am amazed at how few managers seem to know how to *deal with a nonperformer* effectively. More harm is done in this area than in most other facets of managing people. A scolding, the "five-point plan" and threatening workers all lead to poorer performance in the future. The key to dealing with a worker who is not meeting the required standard is to help him, not hammer him.

Give me recognition for my contribution by rewarding me accordingly

If the control system, on the other hand, highlights the fact that a particular worker has performed well, it is only right that management should recognise this and reward him in an appropriate manner. Rewards are not just limited to financial rewards. Some of the most significant rewards are the psychological ones.

The important aspect of rewards is that they must serve to recognise good performance. If, for example, the reward system in an organisation makes little or no distinction between the good and the average performer, it is likely to lead to a climate of mediocrity.

The agenda

It is not nearly as important for a manager to understand a particular theory of motivation as it is to meet these five expectations of his subordinates. The agenda for the rest of this book will therefore be to discuss what each of these five expectations requires of a manager in practice.

13 SETTING OBJECTIVES

An important prerequisite

Before a manager can sit down with a subordinate to agree on the objectives that he will pursue, it may be necessary to look at the way the subordinate's job has been designed. What has to be determined is whether the individual has a "complete" task to do. If a person is the only incumbent doing a particular task, it is likely that he is already in that position, but if there is more than one person involved in the same task, the job may need to be redesigned.

Allocation per product

One of the ways that workers can be given a "defendable territory" that they can identify as their own is to give them specific responsibility for a product or products. Alfred Sloan (1972:45) reorganised General Motors by creating a Buick division, a Chevrolet division, etc. where each division had total responsibility for its production, marketing, financing, etc. instead of having centralised head office divisions carrying out these functions for all the divisions. This allocation per product took place at the highest levels in the organisation, even resulting in the various divisions competing in the market-place. But it gave GM a very strong competitive edge over Ford in the pre-war years.

An example of this type of job design at a lower level was given in chapter 10. The cost controllers of a large manufacturing concern were given the responsibility for the entire calculations on specific products. The result was that workers were able to speak of "my products".

> A farmer in the Vaalharts Irrigation Scheme farmed with potatoes, cabbages, lucerne, sheep and cotton. He had only a handful of workers and they all had to work together in the areas that needed attention.

To give them their own "defendable territory" the farmer put each worker in charge of a particular product. When there was work to be done with the potatoes, they would all work under the direction of the worker in charge of the potatoes. The following week the entire labour force would be working with the sheep under the direction of the worker in charge of the sheep, and so on.

This farmer reported not only a high level of commitment from each of his workers, but also a tremendous amount of cooperation among them. He had made each one "somebody" with respect to a particular product.

Allocation per area

This type of allocation is very common among salespeople. Each salesman is given a particular geographical territory to cover. Another example was the assistant roads foremen mentioned in chapter 10. Each was given responsibility for a specific area, which caused him to speak of "my roads".

In a supermarket shelf packers are often allocated a certain number of gondolas, and they are then measured on aspects such as attractiveness of the merchandising, the number of times they run out of stock on their products, and even on the sales turnover from their areas.

The examples abound. The gardeners at the hospital referred to in chapter 9 were each given a specific area to care for. On the other hand, the workers cutting grass at the side of the road (chapter 8) were not motivated because they were all working in a crowd where nobody's work could be identified as his own.

In one fairly large organisation a team of artisans was responsible for the maintenance of the buildings. The foreman would allocate jobs on a weekly (sometimes daily) basis to whomever was available. However, it was very difficult to measure the performance of the artisans.

To overcome the problem, each artisan (with his team) was given responsibility for the maintenance of a specific section of the buildings. The result was that they could speak of "my section", but it also enabled management to measure the quality of each artisan's work.

Allocation per equipment

Work can also be allocated per equipment. Again, this can be applied very effectively with the maintenance of machinery. In the roads department referred to in chapter 10, the machines (bulldozers, graders, trucks, etc.) were allocated to specific mechanics at the various depots for the regular maintenance work. They soon started taking a pride in their machines and management ran into a new problem when they found that the mechanics were beginning to scold drivers for not looking after their vehicles properly – and there was some confusion about the authority of the mechanics and the authority of the drivers' immediate supervisors.

Allocation per customer

In a building society there was rather low morale in the section that processed mortgage applications. The process involved seven steps and the work was allocated in such a way that Miss A did steps one to three, Miss B did steps four and five, and Miss C did steps six and seven. When "Mr Jones" phoned to enquire about his application, to whom did the telephonist put him through?

The work was redesigned by making each clerk responsible for all seven steps, with Miss A dealing with all clients with surnames A to H, Miss B dealing with I to R and Miss C dealing with S to Z. Not only did the service improve, so did the level of motivation since these clerks were now able to speak of "my clients".

The process of goal setting

There are four steps involved in the process of setting goals with subordinates. It has been my experience that when these four steps are followed carefully, most managers can arrive at meaningful goals with their subordinates, even though for some jobs it is more difficult than for others.

Identifying the performance areas

The question to be answered first is: *In which areas must the job incumbent perform well in order to be successful in this job?*

Some authors call these areas "effectiveness areas" or "key result areas" and they refer to the major outputs that the incumbent has to produce. Ideally there should be no more than seven or eight such areas; otherwise the focus is likely to be on activities rather than on end results.

> The performance areas for a typical machine operator could well be:
> ☐ Volume of production
> ☐ Quality of production
> ☐ Material usage
> ☐ Machine care
> ☐ Safety

The question may be asked whether "costs" should not be another performance area. The answer is negative since costs are already built into the performance areas themselves. If he maximises material usage, looks after his machinery, has a very low accident rate, etc. his costs will automatically be low.

To identify the performance areas of any particular position is not very difficult, but that in itself is not very useful. The performance areas for the machine operator are not yet usable goals since they cannot be measured. We have to go a step further.

Agreeing on the yardsticks

The next question to be answered is: *How will we measure success in each of the performance areas?*

This is undoubtedly the most difficult part of goal setting, and for that reason the appendix lists a number of performance areas and yardsticks that will give some ideas on the type of yardsticks that can be used for different positions. Two questions that will provide some clues are:
☐ What will be the result if he performs poorly?
☐ How do good performers differ from poor ones?

For example, if the machine operator performs poorly with respect to the quality of production, what will the result be? There will be a high reject rate, so the obvious yardstick is *reject rate*.

What would the yardstick for volume of production be? If he is able to produce as many units as he can, the yardstick would obviously be *units per day* (or per month). If, however, he has to produce a fixed quantity, how will a good performer differ from a poor one? The chances are that the poor performer will always be behind schedule, so the most appropriate yardstick would be *unit-days late per month*.

> The yardsticks for a machine operator would probably be as follows:
> ☐ Volume of production
>   — *Units per week, or unit-days late per week*
> ☐ Quality of production
>   — *Reject rate per month*
> ☐ Material usage
>   — *Scrap rate per month*
> ☐ Equipment care
>   — *Breakdown hours per month*
> ☐ Safety
>   — *Number of safety contraventions*

Please note that an *individual* operator's "Safety" is to be measured in terms of the number of times the supervisor has to tell him to put on his gloves, or his goggles, or whatever. Many operators don't bother to adhere to the safety regulations until they are told to do so. If, however, they are scored on how often they have to be told, they soon start obeying the rules.

One of the most crucial considerations in agreeing on yardsticks (note that it is an *agreement*, not an instruction) is whether the incumbent has *control* over the achievement of those results. Does he have the authority to make decisions relating to that performance area? If, for example, he is allowed to decide on how many people to employ in his department, it is perfectly fair to measure his manpower utilisation on *labour costs*. However, if he is given a fixed number of subordinates, it would not be fair to measure him on that aspect and a yardstick like *absenteeism* would be more appropriate.

> An operator on a machine producing copper sheets, had to make adjustments (in response to a visual gauge) to ensure that the thick-

> ness of the copper stayed within the specifications. The best he could achieve, however, was a 40 per cent reject rate.
> Despite additional training and counselling, he could not improve on this figure and eventually he was fired. The same fate befell the next two operators.
> Finally, the general manager of this South African company decided to do the job himself for a few days – and he could not do any better than the operators.
> They had been measured on a yardstick over which they had little control.

It happens quite frequently that in the process of agreeing on yardsticks, deficiencies in the organisation structure come to light. Recently I was helping with the identification of a coal miner's yardsticks when a big discussion arose whether the miner should be measured on the breakdown hours of his machinery or whether that yardstick should be applied to the maintenance crew. During the discussion it became obvious that nobody was quite sure who was responsible for what – and we had to clarify that issue before any progress could be made towards goal-setting.

Another important factor in drawing up yardsticks is that they must be quantifiable. Otherwise it is not possible to set specific goals, and the result is a "do your best" approach. In such cases it becomes impossible to measure work performance objectively.

What happens in cases where work performance is difficult to measure quantitatively? A typical example is housekeeping on the shop floor, that is, how neatly the work-place is kept. Other examples would be the quality of the roads in the assistant road foreman's area, or the attractiveness of the hospital gardens.

In such cases the manager's subjective evaluation must be expressed in terms of a rating, for example, a point out of 10. This form of measurement is not ideal, but it is certainly better than no measurement at all.

It is an established fact that *what you measure is what you get*. A good example is the case of the loaders at the sugar estate overloading the trucks because that is what they were being measured on (see chapter 9). It may, therefore, be necessary to use more than one yardstick per performance area in order to ensure a balanced emphasis. If only quantity is measured, quality is very likely to suffer. If only mistakes are measured, the work pace is likely to slow down.

> At a coal mine near Middelburg, the miners are paid a bonus on the number of coal-faces they blast and haul away per shift. They are not measured on how much coal they mine with each blast.
> As a result, they often blast less coal per face in order to achieve more "faces" – and thus get paid more.
> What you measure is what you get!

Budgets as a form of measurement can very easily bring about poor management practices. For example, the project manager of a large manufacturing company told me that in his organisation they were measured on how close their actual expenses came to budget. On one particular project he could easily have saved half a million rands, but then he stood a good chance of being reprimanded for budgeting poorly. So he built the extra costs into the project.

A divisional manager of the same company told me that one year he had budgeted for sales of R12 million, but that his team had sold R20 million. When the managing director called him in, he expected to be praised (maybe even promoted). Imagine his sheer disbelief when he was reprimanded for having budgeted so poorly, since his sales had thrown production schedules into disarray! His reaction was to budget for R16 million the following year. When that target was reached, he instructed his staff to stop selling or hold orders over for the next year.

> In a building society a branch manager had an amount of R7 000 in his budget for travelling expenses. This was for reimbursing staff who used their own vehicles for official business.
> It was an insignificant amount, but the attitude of top management was that if any manager exceeded his expense budget, "it would be taken into account at the next salary review".
> One day the manager received a call from a farmer who wanted to invest R100 000 in the building society and asked the manager if someone could come to give him some investment advice and at the same time pick up the cheque.
> The manager quickly estimated that this would cost about R70 in travelling expenses and that this would bring him dangerously close to his limit. He therefore told the client that there was nobody

> available at the moment, but that he would ask the agent (the local attorney) in the town nearby to come out to the farm.
> The agent advised the client, paid the money into the branch account, and the manager felt very pleased with himself for having saved R70 on his expenses. However, the agent received a commission of R500.
> What you measure is what you get!

A far more effective method of budgeting would have been in terms of a ratio. For example, the expense of obtaining money (whether it is agents' commission or travelling costs) should not exceed a certain percentage of the money that has been brought in. Then it could be left to the discretion of the manager to determine the most economic method. However, ratio budgets are unpopular – especially with accountants because they like fixed figures.

The accounting system is probably one of the most powerful forces that shapes the behaviour in an organisation. The regional manager of a large timber company, for example, found it very difficult to implement the human resource approach because of the accountants at head office. He wanted to start monitoring the performance of his district managers by measuring only the results in the key performance areas and only in those cases where the results showed a downward trend would he start scrutinising the finer details. Furthermore, he accepted the fact that seasonal fluctuations caused the bottom line to vary from month to month. As long as the general trend showed that the district manager was on target towards achieving the annual goal, the regional manager would not interfere.

However, head office accountants worked on a monthly profit and loss figure, and as soon as the figures for one particular month were down, or there was a rather high expense item in a certain area, they would report it immediately to the managing director. The MD would demand to know the reason from the divisional manager, who would question the regional manager, who in turn questioned the district manager, who in turn questioned the area manager.

The whole management process in that company had developed into an exercise of manipulating the figures to keep head office happy and in the process all management autonomy and effective decision making went by the board.

Establish the historical performance levels

The next question to be answered is: *What was the performance level in the past for each of the yardsticks?*

We must put figures to the yardsticks. We cannot just suck them out of our thumbs. Where do we get the figures from? By reviewing the historical performance levels.

Since the most effective competition is always against oneself, the most meaningful goal to chase is the previous performance level. If no records of past performance exist, a manager has four options:

☐ He can measure the actual performance over a period of time to establish the norm.
— *The head of the computer operators (see chapter 9) measured the performance of each shift over a period of two weeks.*

☐ He can make use of time-and-motion study.
— *This is an expensive method that does not necessarily give more accurate figures, and is sometimes seen by workers as being "unfair".*

☐ He can find some other source to compare with, for example, an industry average.
— *This may not always be a valid figure since the conditions in a particular company may be very different from those of other organisations.*

☐ He can take an educated guess as to what would be acceptable performance. The actual measurement will soon confirm how valid the estimate was.
— *The station master (see chapter 9) estimated that it would take six months to clean up the place.*

The historical performance levels tell us what happened in the past. But what do they tell us about the future? Those figures are an indication of what we can expect in the future *if we continue doing the same things*. If we carry on as usual, we can expect similar levels of performance on the assumption that the external conditions will also be relatively similar. This brings us to one of the most critical aspects of the management task, and that is to stimulate continuous improvement – but that will be dealt with in the next chapter.

Agreeing on the goals

The last question to be answered in the process of setting objectives with subordinates is: *What figure should we aim for in the future?*

It is important at this stage to distinguish between *volume* goals and *quality* goals. Volume goals refer to *increases* in output, e.g. higher sales, more accounts, increased production, etc. These figures tell us what the magnitude of the business is likely to be.

Quality goals, on the other hand, refer to *improvement* in products, service, methods, etc. These goals must also be expressed in numerical terms, but the actual goal should be to *improve on the historical performance levels*. It doesn't matter whether the improvement is large or small – what is important is to establish a process of continuing improvement as a way of life. That means each year we have to be performing better in terms of the quality of our entire operation.

Tom Peters stresses throughout his challenging and thought-provoking book *Thriving on chaos* (1988:276) that successful companies never stop their efforts to improve every aspect of their business. They will celebrate every improvement, but they never sit back with the feeling that they have arrived.

When it comes to volume goals, however, it *is* necessary to aim for specific figures, otherwise the planning and coordinating functions will suffer severely. It would, for example, be impossible to do any meaningful budgeting.

Such goals are always limited to a period of time – usually one year – and will vary from situation to situation, and from subordinate to subordinate. The performance areas and yardsticks for the branch managers of a retail organisation will probably be the same, but the actual goals for each branch will vary according to its location, its size and the branch manager's expertise. It is important to understand that everyone must compete against himself and not against somebody else. That is why historical performance records are an important basis for setting future targets. Each branch, each vehicle, each sales area, etc. must compete against its own previous performance levels.

The fact that the goals are annual goals does not mean that they are measured only once a year. Measurement and feedback are ongoing processes. An annual goal, however, allows for fluctuations in performance. Not achieving a target in a particular week or month does not mean that the subordinate has failed. It simply means that he will have to perform better in the future in order to achieve his annual goal.

A second very important aspect to take into account when setting goals is that *low goals are more motivating than high goals*.

> One of the five large building societies in South Africa had set a goal of 9 per cent growth for seven years in a row. And for seven years they achieved an average growth of 6 per cent – the lowest of the five major building societies.

> How did that affect the branch managers and their staff? Anybody who fails seven years in a row will be discouraged, and each new year when top management set a 9 per cent goal they would say: "Yes, Sir, we think it's possible," but with little enthusiasm since they "knew" they wouldn't be able to achieve it.
>
> Then a new marketing manager was appointed. In his first year he set the goal at 6 per cent. The branch managers laughed at him and told him that that would be easy to achieve. In fact the target was reached in the eighth month of the financial year.
>
> However, instead of sitting back they said: "Now we'll show the old man what we can really do." They ended the year with a growth of 9,2 per cent – the second highest of all the building societies.
>
> The following year the marketing manager set the goal at 9 per cent, and they achieved 6 per cent. Why? Because one year's success was not sufficient to wipe out the impact of seven years of failure.
>
> I cannot prove it, but my guess is that if he had allowed them to set the goal themselves, they would possibly have aimed for a 7 per cent growth and achieved 10 per cent.

It is a myth in the business world that high goals motivate people. They do not. High goals that are imposed on subordinates are far more likely to demotivate them. If, for example, a manager tells a subordinate that he can achieve more, it arouses a subconscious desire in the subordinate to prove his boss wrong. Of course, it works the other way round as well.

A fertiliser company asked its salesmen to set their own sales targets. One representative set himself the goal of selling 15 000 tons in one year. However, his geographical sales area was reduced, and the general manager called him in to explain the reasons and to tell him that his sales target had been reduced to 12 000 tons.

He was quite indignant that they thought he couldn't sell 15 000 tons even though his area was a little smaller. To prove to them how wrong they were, he sold 18 000 tons that year.

The key to understanding the role of goals in motivating others is the fact that goals must increase the likelihood of success. By a "low goal" I mean a realistic goal where the likelihood of success is very good. "A sense of achievement" is synonymous with "an experience of success", and by lowering the goals the likelihood of success provides the motivating force.

Parents do their children a great disservice by pushing for high marks at school. It is more effective to lower a child's goals – he would love to prove his parents wrong.

> A father told me that he had forced his son to come to his office each afternoon to do his homework there. Despite this strict supervision his son failed every subject in the first term of standard 9. Instead of giving him a good thrashing, he decided to follow my advice. He apologised to his son for putting him under so much pressure and acknowledged that he was gifted mechanically and not academically.
>
> He asked his son to set his own goals for the next term, and the boy aimed for an average of just over 40 per cent. The father accepted this goal and put the full responsibility for homework on his son. This meant that it was his decision whether to study or not. However, they agreed that if he did not achieve the marks *he* said he would, the father would have to curtail his sport activities and his television viewing.
>
> The next term the son achieved all his goals and for the first time his dad praised him rather than scolded him for his schoolwork. He passed standard 9 at the end of the year with an average of 55 per cent.
>
> The next year he passed his matric exams with two Bs, two Cs, and two Ds. That's a good first-class pass, and he went on to enrol at a technikon for a diploma in mechanical engineering.
>
> It is dangerous to say to a child: "I know you can do much better." The child might just be tempted to prove you wrong.

Although a manager may have to set the initial goals for a subordinate, it is always better for the subordinate to set the goals himself. If the subordinate sets a relatively low (but acceptable) goal, it should not be increased. The chances that the actual result will be much higher are very good.

The fear that a subordinate will set an extremely low goal is ungrounded. Most subordinates, when told the historical performance level, will want to improve on that. More often than not subordinates are inclined to set themselves extremely high goals. In that case the manager must encourage them to pursue those high goals, but he must indicate a lower level with which he will be satisfied.

Another project team in the timber company referred to earlier set themselves the very ambitious target of completing a project in less than 100 days. Their superior realised that the goal was too high, but he did not lower it.

The project was a huge success, saving the company something like R2 million a year, but it took 102 days to complete.

The result? Every team member experienced an abject sense of failure – because of a manager's failure to lower the goal.

An important principle in setting objectives is that subordinates must be told explicitly that they are allowed to make a certain number of mistakes. Most managers are horrified at this idea. When I ask them how many mistakes their subordinates are allowed to make, they usually say "none". That means that they are demanding perfection of their subordinates, and only "perfect" managers have the right to do that.

Insisting on a perfect score means that a subordinate fails if he makes only one or two small mistakes. Making allowances for a certain number of mistakes creates a much stronger motivation to achieve "zero defects" than to make no allowances for it. The subordinate must believe that he has a good chance of being successful.

What about budgets?

I have come across many managers who believe that they are managing by objectives because they set annual, quarterly and even monthly budgets. A budget is obviously a form of goal setting, but it does not cover the full spectrum because it tends to focus mainly on the cost aspect. Sales budgets and production budgets usually include output targets, but the same cannot be said for some of the other functions in the organisation. Of the 87 yardsticks listed in the appendix, at least 75 would not be covered by a budget.

Budgets must be seen as only one facet of the objective-setting process.

In conclusion

For certain jobs it is very difficult to distinguish between the work performance of individual workers. For example, two or three drivers may be assigned to a specific vehicle on a shift basis. In such a case the objectives can be set for the team as a whole – although a team should preferably not exceed ten members. If one team member is bringing down the team's overall performance by his poor work, the others will soon begin to exert pressure on him to shape up.

Throughout the process of objective setting the emphasis must always be on *agreement* between manager and subordinate. However, if they cannot reach consensus, the final authority will always rest with the manager. Involving subordinates in the decision-making process does not imply that the manager loses his authority. In the final analysis he is the one accountable for the results of his unit.

14 PARTICIPATION AND DELEGATION

"If only he had asked me"

The second expectation that a subordinate has of his manager is to give him an opportunity to prove himself. When a manager, for example, gives the wrong solution to a problem, or comes up with a plan that doesn't work, his subordinates will often say to themselves: "If only he had asked me, I could have told him it wouldn't work." But by then it's too late, because the manager will be very reluctant to back down and admit that he made a mistake.

"I wish the boss would leave me alone"

Managers also have the tendency to interfere with the work of their subordinates. They believe that subordinates are there to help the manager get the work done, and in the process the managers take the responsibility for the work on themselves, by telling the subordinates what to do. This robs the subordinate of the opportunity of proving what he is capable of.

Subordinates want help and assistance while they are still in the learning stages, but after that they want to be given an opportunity to prove themselves. This can be done in two ways:
☐ Participation in decision making
☐ Delegation of responsibility

Participation in decision making

One way of giving subordinates an opportunity to prove themselves is to involve them in the decision-making process, that is, to consult them, to ask them for solutions, to bring them in on problem-solving discussions.

Peters and Waterman (1984:200) identified *innovation* as one of the major factors contributing to the success of America's top companies. They give numerous examples of successful organisations that are continually introducing new products, new materials, new uses for existing products, etc. If we analyse the reasons for the success of some of South Africa's top entrepreneurs, we find that most of them took the initiative to come up with something new (Ball & Asbury 1989:111).

> Very few entrepreneurs would have risked investing millions in a place like Sun City, which is in the middle of nowhere, far from any metropolitan centre. Yet Sol Kerzner took the initiative and it turned out a huge financial success.

Innovation is, however, not limited to entrepreneurs or top management. It can be introduced at all levels in the organisation. The examples given in chapter 10 confirm that workers at the lowest levels can come up with ideas for improvement, both large and small.

> The marketing team of a toothpaste company held an in-depth discussion on what they could do to increase the sales of toothpaste. After the meeting the marketing manager gave his secretary a long list of proposals to type out.
> When she had completed the task, she told him that there was a much simpler way. Since people usually put toothpaste on the full length of the toothbrush, they would increase the use of toothpaste if the opening of the toothpaste tube was larger.
> Most toothpaste tubes these days have larger openings – and the sales have gone up.

In the above examples the innovation came by chance as a "flash insight". A concerted effort must, however, be made by the manager and his subordinates to determine the factors that contribute to the performance level, and what can be done to improve them.

It is true that performance can sometimes be improved by training and motivating the worker concerned – but it is just as true that the problem could lie with the *machines* that have to be operated, or with the *materials* that have to be used, or with the *methods* that have to be followed.

To stimulate innovation there are three key questions that need to be asked:
- What can we do *differently*?
- What can we do *additionally*?
- What can we *stop* doing?

What can we do differently?

At the assembly plant of one of South Africa's car manufacturers the body of each vehicle moved along the assembly line on a bogie (a kind of trolley) until it was ready to be placed on the chassis. An operator then had to push each bogie from the end of the production line back to the beginning – a distance of 131 m. In the process he walked an average of 14,3 km a day (from Durban to Cape Town and back in a year).

However, the workers are continually challenged by management to think of better ways of doing things. As a result, the operator who had to push the bogies came up with the idea of taking a jack trolley, extending the arms and loading three bogies at a time. He now walks 5 km a day.

Another example was the removal of the plastic backing from a self-adhesive clip. Eight such clips had to be put on each vehicle. It was time-consuming to remove this plastic backing, and the worker had to have long nails. The operator responsible for this task had the idea of taking a thick roll of masking tape and pressing the clip with the plastic backing onto it. When lifted off, the backing remained behind. The time taken to perform this task was reduced by more than half.

What can we do additionally?

Small retailers often find it difficult to compete with the large departmental stores as far as price is concerned, yet they can still be very successful by simply providing that extra bit of personalised service that the chain stores cannot give.

A pharmacist in a large city took the trouble to phone each person who had bought prescription medicine from him. He simply asked how the patient was doing and whether the medicine had helped. Not only did he gain valuable insight into the benefits of various medicines, but he also found that his turnover increased in non-medicine lines like cosmetics.

A ladies' hairdressing salon used an instant camera to take a photograph of every client's hairdo when it was completed. This was kept on file and the next time the client came in the photograph would be used as a basis to decide how her hair was to be done. They could barely keep up with the increase in customers.

What can we stop doing?

In most large organisations a great deal of unnecessary work is performed with monotonous regularity. Activities that made sense in the past often become redundant as new systems are introduced.

In one of South Africa's large insurance companies a manager was appointed as head of a particular department. He called in the staff one by one to get to know them a little better and to find out what their duties were. One woman told him that for the past ten years she had kept records of all the different types of policies sold to different age groups. She told him that she filed her work in a cabinet, but was unable to tell him who made use of these figures.

After making enquiries the manager discovered that ten years before the general manager had asked: "How many people under the age of 25 buy a Table VII policy?" When they could not give him an immediate answer, he reprimanded them severely. The result was that they immediately appointed someone to keep such records.

That general manager was fired four years later. The new general manager was unaware of the existence of these figures; nor was he particularly interested in them. Yet the task was done month by month. That is known as JIC management – "just in case"!

The branch manager of a building society told me that he became so fed up with all the reports and statistics that he had to send to head office each month that he instructed his staff to stop sending them. Seven months later someone at head office phoned to ask him where the figures were. It was the filing clerk at head office. She had noticed the gap.

At a management seminar in Johannesburg I was told by one of the participants that his company produced leather goods for the defence force. At the time they were manufacturing mainly aircraft seats. One of the specifications was that the leather had to be soaked in horse manure and urine for two days. One day someone queried this and it was discovered that many years ago they had produced saddles for the army. The soaking was done to give the leather a familiar smell so that the horses would not spook when a new saddle was put on them.

Perhaps the answer to the question: "What can we stop doing?" is simply: "Nothing", but the question must be asked frequently. Nothing must become a "sacred cow" in the organisation. Continuous improvement must be measured on an ongoing basis – and every improvement, no matter how small, must be celebrated. Peters (1988:276) gives an overwhelming number of examples of successful companies that are obsessed with improvement. It has become a way of life for them.

> I sometimes ask top managers to tell me how many improvements their employees have introduced in the last six months. I also ask them how they measure these improvements and how they celebrate them.
> Most of them don't know what I'm talking about.

Where do the best ideas come from?

Why is it important to get employees thinking? In chapter 10 we talked about the commitment that it created in the individuals who were "investing their egos" in solutions that they had generated; but another important reason is the fact that workers often come up with the best ideas – simply because they see the situation from a different perspective.

> The story is told of an office block in Chicago that had insufficient elevators. People were constantly having to queue for the elevators in the banking hall downstairs. The only solution was to build another elevator by knocking a hole through every floor.
> While the engineers and architects were taking all kinds of measurements, the janitor asked what they were doing. When they told him, he was visibly upset about the mess it would create, for he was very proud of his clean building.
> He off-handedly commented that he wouldn't put an elevator there, and when the engineer rather cynically asked him where he would put it, the janitor said: "I would build it outside."
> This led to the first "outside" elevator in the world, and made the building a well-known tourist attraction, not to mention the tremendous savings in building costs.

More perspiration than inspiration

Thomas Edison is reported to have said that creativity involves 5 per cent inspiration and 95 per cent perspiration. And he was right. Most managers are dependent on the "flash-insights" that one gets while driving or taking a shower, but it requires a concerted and sustained effort to get people to think for themselves. In chapter 10 I referred to the tremendous number of creative ideas that are being generated by operators at a car manufacturing plant. This was achieved only through the appointment of two men at a senior level who initiated all kinds of programmes to stimulate creative thinking – and it was several years before it really took off.

> Compare this with a construction company in South Africa which insists that every employee must sign an undertaking that if they ever come up with a new idea or patent while employed by the company, it will become the property of the company.
>
> The effect of that policy is that very few employees bother to experiment with new ideas since they have nothing to gain; right from the start management quashes the potential creativity of their subordinates.
>
> One employee, however, thought of a method to prevent expensive jackhammer drills from breaking in the ground. Knowing that he could never benefit from the idea while he stayed with the company, he immediately resigned and formed his own company.
>
> He is now a wealthy businessman, supplying drills to his previous employer. If they hadn't persisted with their foolish policy, he could have been given a suitable reward and probably still be in their employ today.
>
> The short-sightedness of some managers never ceases to amaze me.

Stimulating subordinates to think for themselves is not easy. Many a manager has gone to his subordinates with a problem and asked them: "What do you think we should do?" When he didn't get an answer immediately, he would suggest the solution himself. The result is that the workers are still not thinking for themselves.

Workers who have never been asked to think will not start doing so overnight. It takes a great deal of patience. One Free State farmer told his workers that in future none of them was allowed to report a problem unless he also suggested a solution. For the next few weeks they would report problems to him and when he asked them the solution they would say that they didn't know. Instead of solving it, he would say: "Go and think about it and then come back to me." (No problem is so urgent that it cannot wait for an hour or two.) It took three to four months before the workers started thinking for themselves, but today they have the confidence to deal with numerous problems on their own, giving him a lot more free time.

The cost of "waste"

A particularly fruitful area for improvement is the elimination of "waste" – and by that I do not mean only the waste in materials – but rather the waste in unnecessary effort. It is estimated that the cost of doing things over that should have been done right in the first place runs as high as 35 to 40 per cent of total cost in South African companies. The corresponding figure in Japanese companies is about 5 per cent.

> A recent analysis at a plant of one of South Africa's top companies brought to light that their cost of "waste" was R90 m per annum. And that was in a top company!

One of the major reasons for such a high figure is that very few companies bother to measure this "cost of waste", let alone take active steps to eliminate it.

In chapter 10 I described the successes achieved by a motor manufacturing plant in "creating thinking workers". Much of their focus has been on the elimination of "waste", using, amongst others, a waste questionnaire to stimulate the thinking of their workers. For them, improvement is an on-going way of life.

The problem of communication

Many books have been written about the skill of communication, and I suppose there is some truth to the fact that some people are more skilled at communicating than others. Some seem to have an ability to say the right thing at the right time and have a very good command of the language, while others don't even realise how confusing their instructions can be.

> I actually heard a builder doing some work at our house, say to one of his subordinates: "Alfeus, take the bakkie and pick up the cement at the store. Hurry up and drive slowly!"

I have an idea that this manager's subordinates no longer bother to listen to what the boss is saying. Nobody will dispute the importance of communicating clearly and explaining issues lucidly, but I don't think that that is the real problem when it comes to communicating.

The problem is not *how well* managers communicate but *that* they communicate. It's not that managers don't know how to share management information with their subordinates; they just don't bother to do so. Yet communication has a tremendous impact on subordinates.

> The managing director of a small company in the Cape tends to explain things in a very roundabout way. He often struggles to find the right words to express his ideas.
>
> Yet his communication with his subordinates is of a very high standard simply because he takes the trouble to hold regular management meetings and inform his staff of what is happening in the company.

A good example of a manager making the effort to communicate is the station master (see chapter 10) who holds weekly meetings with all his employees (even at the lowest level) and shares management information with them. I don't know how skilled he is with words, but I do know that his communication as a manager is superb because he takes the trouble to communicate.

> My experience as a marriage counsellor has confirmed that the problem of communication between a husband and wife is very seldom the fact that they don't know how to communicate – it is mostly a problem of not being *willing* to communicate.

So often managers don't communicate because they take it for granted that the subordinates "know" what to do. A company that supplied automotive parts to a car manufacturer received complaints that the number of faulty parts were exceptionally high. Investigations confirmed that this was indeed so and management were perplexed since they had very sophisticated equipment that tested each part that was shipped to the manufacturer.

It took them three months to discover that although the ten operators had been taught very carefully how to identify faulty parts, management had not instructed them specifically to put the faulty parts in a reject pile. Consequently two of the operators had been putting the faulty parts with the good ones and sending them off to the customer.

> Before you jump to conclusions about "typically stupid operators" – it was a company in Britain.

Some practical suggestions

How does a manager set about involving his subordinates in problem solving? He must schedule regular meetings, say once a week, where the key innovation questions are asked:
☐ What can we do *differently?*
☐ What can we do *additionally?*
☐ What can we *stop* doing?

If the manager also tells each subordinate that he will be expected to make some suggestions at the next meeting, it puts pressure on the workers to start thinking for themselves. However, this type of meeting focuses on innovation, that is, ways to do things more efficiently. It does not necessarily address problem areas.

A manager should also call in his subordinates whenever there is a particular problem that affects them. (It is important that only those workers who are directly affected be involved. Nothing is more frustrating than attending a meeting where the topic of discussion is unrelated to one's own situation.)

Although some people are naturally skilled at leading such discussions and getting everyone involved, most managers could become a great deal more effective if they stick strictly to the following agenda:

What is the problem?

☐ It is important that the initial discussion should focus on defining the problem and not on proposing solutions. If the problem is not defined correctly, the result may be the right answer for the wrong problem. "Poor motivation" may, for example, be seen as the cause of low labour productivity, but if the real problem is "poor training", the solution to solve the poor motivation problem will not be very effective.

☐ The most important role of a leader is to ensure that the discussion focuses on one topic at a time. He may, for example, have to say: "That sounds like a good idea, Joe, but let's clarify the problem before we discuss any solutions." The problem must be thoroughly analysed before any solutions are discussed.

What are the alternatives?

☐ A characteristic of so many problem-solving discussions is that most of the participants will decide very quickly for themselves what the solution should be and then spend the rest of the time trying to convince the other participants. The result is that not much time is spent on generating creative solutions, since each person is emotionally committed to defending his own point of view. It is, therefore, extremely important that all the possibilities should be listed before they are discussed.

☐ The brain performs two basic functions. It can be creative and it can be evaluative, but it cannot exercise both functions at the same time. Most of us are inclined to be evaluative, that is, consider each proposal critically, but in the process we quash the creative function. A very useful technique to set aside the evaluative function for a while is *brainstorming*. This is a simple technique whereby *all ideas* are written on a board (regardless of whether they are "stupid" or have been stated before). *No comment* is allowed until all the ideas have run dry – and the leader must allow plenty of time for this.

What are the pros and cons?

☐ The evaluative function of the brain is only put into gear after a list of all the alternatives has been drawn up. This critical evaluation involves writing down the advantages and disadvantages of *each alternative.* Only then is the group in a position to decide on the solution.

☐ Some years ago I assisted a company in appointing a new general manager. There were three candidates on the short list and, after the board of directors had interviewed each one, I asked them who their choice was. Some directors argued for candidate A because he had some very strong points in his favour, but also some serious shortcomings. Others argued for candidate B who had other strengths in his favour, but also some major shortcomings. I then listed the strengths and weaknesses of all three candidates on a flip chart and to my amazement the board unanimously decided to appoint candidate C. He didn't have such outstanding characteristics, but he had many strengths and very few shortcomings for that position.

Strive for consensus

☐ It is relatively simple for a group to reach a decision by taking a majority vote, or accepting the proposals of the "dominant minority" (e.g. the boss), but in the process a number of the team members may be alienated, and certainly not very committed to the solution.

☐ Consensus implies that every member of the group agrees (at least to some extent) that there is no better alternative. That means that the leader must ensure that *everybody's opinions* are listened to and discussed to their logical conclusion.

Effective leadership as far as problem solving is concerned does not mean that the leader has to come up with the best ideas. Effective leadership implies the ability to utilise the ideas of others and to create a strong commitment to teamwork.

Remember: the yardstick for a successful leader is not how good he is, but how good his subordinates are.

Who should be involved?

There are several types of groups that must be involved in problem-solving. Firstly, a manager and an individual subordinate can and should be involved in generating improvements in the subordinate's own job. Secondly, a manager should hold innovation discussions with the natural work group, that is, the people who work closely together in a particular section. Sometimes it is necessary to involve the entire department, because the changes will affect other sections in the department.

But even that is not enough. Frequently the problems are of such a nature that people from other departments are involved. A change in one department often necessitates changes in other departments. Such interfunctional groups should actively be encouraged and a quality circle can meet this need very effectively.

What is delegation?

The second way in which a manager can give a subordinate the opportunity to prove himself is to delegate responsibility to him. But what is delegation in the management sense of the word? Let's take an example.

The managing director of a large construction firm phones the industrial relations manager and asks him to find out how many grievances they had to deal with the previous year. The IR manager then goes to one of his subordinates who has such statistics on file and asks him to let the managing director have this figure as soon as possible. Is this an example of delegation? No!

The above example is merely an instruction and there is nothing wrong with giving an instruction of this kind. It just isn't delegation. Why not?

Delegation of responsibility is giving a subordinate the authority to use his own judgment. If an instruction does not require the subordinate to make a decision or use his own discretion, it is not true delegation.

Let's take another example. The manager goes on leave and delegates the running of his department to one of his subordinates. That would certainly require the subordinate to use his judgment, but who makes the decisions once the boss comes back again? The manager. Although it is a sound management practice to put a subordinate in charge, this is only temporary delegation.

Delegation implies that it becomes a permanent part of the subordinate's job. This is not to say that delegating authority for a short period of time is in any way poor management. It can be an excellent development process for the subordinate concerned. However, it is not delegation in the true sense of the word because the decision-making responsibility was not delegated downwards; the subordinate was moved temporarily upwards into the manager's position.

A last example: a factory manager delegates the planning of the production schedule to the assistant manager, but wants to approve it himself before it is put into action. Quite often he changes some of the details on the plan. Again, this is not real delegation.

Delegation implies that a manager is subject to the authority of his subordinate on the aspect that was delegated. The factory manager in the example has broken one of the cardinal rules that apply to delegating responsibility. Two people cannot be responsible for the same thing. Either the manager makes the decisions or his subordinate does, but whoever makes the decisions is the one who has the responsibility.

> Many managers insist on checking and signing all letters written by their subordinates, in the process often changing the way something has been said in the letter rather than correcting the factual information. That is poor management!
> Either the subordinate is incompetent to write letters and should be trained to do so, or the manager should write the letters himself and let the subordinate spend his time more profitably. They cannot both be responsible for writing letters.

Some managers would defend the above criticism on the grounds that they need to be kept informed. That's a fair argument, but then they can merely ask to see a copy of the letter that has been signed by the person who wrote it.

In cases where there is a legal or policy requirement that the manager signs the letter, he can agree with the subordinate to "sign blind" so that the full responsibility rests on the subordinate. Of course, this means that a manager dare not delegate such responsibility unless the subordinate is competent to handle it.

Responsibility versus accountability

The question of whether a manager can delegate responsibility or not has been debated for many years. Responsibility is often confused with accountability – and nobody seems to know the difference. It is, however, only an academic difference – that's why most of the academics cannot agree. Let's use an example to illustrate it.

The marketing manager of a fairly large organisation goes to the advertising manager (one of his subordinates) and tells him that he is responsible for the advertising campaign. He has R300 000 available in the budget and he has to decide on the theme, the media, etc. This is no problem for the subordinate. After all, he is the advertising manager.

He goes to the assistant advertising manager, however, and tells him that it would be good experience for him to handle the entire advertising campaign. The assistant advertising manager then goes to his secretary and tells her that she is far more creative than he is and that he would like her to plan the advertising campaign. She in turn goes to the office messenger and tells him that since they sell such a large volume of their products to black people, he will know far better than she what adverts will appeal to their potential customers. She tells him that he has R300 000 in his budget and that he must make the necessary decisions and handle the negotiations with the advertising agency.

This is a very far-fetched example, but who is *responsible* at this stage for the advertising campaign? The messenger. He is the one who has to make the decisions. What nobody knows, however, is that this messenger is doing his doctorate in advertising through Unisa. (He stayed on as messenger simply because it gives him so much spare time for his studies.) The result is that he initiates an extremely successful advertising campaign.

Will the marketing manager mind who made the decisions? No – as long as the project is successful. But what if it is a complete shambles? Who is called in to give account? The advertising manager, of course. He is accountable. That is why a manager can delegate responsibility but not his accountability.

Having grasped this point, consider the next wrinkle. The marketing manager finds that the wrong letters are delivered to him quite frequently. Who is responsible? The messenger. But who is accountable? Some will say the secretary, but it is in fact the messenger who is also accountable. Why is he responsible but not accountable when it comes to the advertising campaign, yet both responsible and accountable when it comes to delivering letters?

The answer is simple. "Letter delivery" is one of the performance areas of the messenger's job. "Advertising" is one of the performance areas of the advertising manager's job. *Responsibility* is, therefore, related to the person who makes the decisions. *Accountability* is related to the job incumbent's performance area. If this were not so, the managing director would ultimately be accountable for everything that happened in the organisation, including wrong delivery of letters – and that would be ridiculous.

What are the advantages of delegation?

It's all very well to argue about the implication of true delegation, but why should managers delegate? There are two basic advantages. The first advantage is that it gives a manager *time*. Time to plan the future rather than organise the present. Time to be *proactive* rather than reactive.

A manager who functions reactively is one who is constantly reacting to the things happening around him – a crisis, a problem, a request, a schedule, etc. A proactive manager not only deals with the problems and programmes that need his attention; he is continually looking ahead to what he can do to prevent future problems. He is constantly thinking about the things he needs to do today in order to be ready for tomorrow. That kind of planning needs a great deal of uninterrupted time and the only way a manager can find that kind of time is to delegate the day-to-day running of the business to his subordinates.

> In their book *The winning streak* authors Goldsmith and Clutterbuck (1985:41) say that one of the characteristics of successful British companies is that they delegate authority down to the lowest levels in the organisation. This leaves top management free to concentrate on the strategic decisions. Lord Charles Forte of Trusthouse Forte, an international catering and hotel group, says for example: "When I expanded to a second milk bar I had to leave a woman in charge of the first. She ran it better than I did. If I hadn't given her her head, I wouldn't have 40 000 employees now. I'd still have twelve."

Ball and Asbury (1989:15) found that the top managers in South Africa's most successful companies gave themselves considerable "mental space". Most of them have deliberately withdrawn themselves from the daily operating activities so that they can concentrate on the enterprise's corporate strategy.

Delegating also gives a manager the time to concentrate on issues that require his personal expertise and/or attention. Some years ago I was head of personnel at a large insurance company. At the time there was a great need to identify employees with management potential while they were still in clerical positions. However, I was so caught up in the day-to-day running of the department that I could not find the time for developing such a system, and none of my subordinates had the necessary expertise.

When some offices a few doors away became vacant, I decided to move physically out of the personnel department and to appoint my deputy as the unofficial department head. I then informed my boss that, if he needed anything done in the department, he should speak to my deputy. If he was unhappy about anything, he should speak to me. I had delegated my responsibility but not my accountability. The result was that I was able to introduce a very effective assessment and development programme, while my deputy proved his competence in managing the personnel department. In due course both of us were promoted. The point is that delegation enabled me as a manager to focus on the issues that required my personal attention.

The second advantage of delegating is the positive effect it has on the subordinates. It affects their level of *competence*. So often managers tell me that they would love to delegate, but that they cannot do so because their subordinates are not competent. My reply to that is: "How will they become competent?"

> Most managers can look back on their own careers and testify to the fact that they learnt the most when they were thrown into the deep end.
> When subordinates are subjected to a "sink or swim" approach, most of them come up swimming.

Delegation also affects the subordinates' level of *confidence*. There is only one way in which any person can ever become confident about his abilities, and that is by experiencing success. If people are not given the opportunity, how can they ever experience that success?

It also affects their level of *motivation*. When subordinates are allowed to use their own judgment to deal with a situation, there is a very strong need to do it well – their pride is at stake.

> One of the most amazing incidents that I have come across was a supervisor who was put in charge of a team of packers. For the first two weeks she decided to work with them to get to know what the work really entailed.
> Within a few days she could see a way of doing things much more efficiently, but she kept quiet and she encouraged the packers to look out for a better way since: "You people know the work far better than I do."

> A week later one of the packers suggested the improvement that the supervisor had identified earlier on. The implementation brought a tremendous change in the attitude of the packers. They produced more and more ideas and they were obviously very proud that "their" ideas were being listened to.
>
> I doubt if I would have had the patience to keep quiet so that my subordinates could have the thrill of using their own judgment. No wonder she was such an outstanding supervisor!

Obstacles to delegation

If delegation has so many advantages, why are managers so reluctant to delegate decision-making responsibility to their subordinates? I want to suggest six basic reasons:

Fear of losing control over the operations

It is important for a manager to know what is going on in his department or section. After all, he is in charge – he must keep his finger on the pulse and the "best" way to do that is make the day-to-day decisions himself.

> Some years ago the general manager of one of the large building societies insisted on opening all incoming mail at head office. His excuse was that it kept him in touch with what was going on.

I have no argument with the fact that a manager must keep in touch, but there are other, more effective, ways of doing that. One of the reasons managers keep interfering with the activities of their subordinates is that they have no other way of assessing their performance and keeping informed of what is going on. This highlights once again the importance of setting measurable goals against which the performance of subordinates can be monitored.

Delegating authority without measuring the end result is abdication and that would be courting disaster. I have quoted many success stories, but there have also been cases of failures where managers have started to implement the human resource theory without success. There seem to be two major reasons for this failure. One of them is the absence of a formal control system (dealt with in chapter 15). The other one is the "dumping" of responsibility on subordinates.

> The situational leadership theory of Hersey and Blanchard (1982) provides excellent insight into and advice for delegating. Their theory is that the amount of responsibility that can be delegated to an individual worker depends on the *task maturity* of that worker. If the individual has a low level of task maturity, the manager has to do a great deal of task structuring and can give very little decision-making responsibility to that subordinate. If, on the other hand, the subordinate has a high level of task maturity, the manager can leave a great deal to that subordinate's discretion.

If a subordinate is, therefore, not yet task mature (i.e. not fully trained), the manager dare not give him the full decision-making responsibility. With competent subordinates, however, a manager should keep control by measuring the end result and not by making all decisions himself.

Risk of subordinates making costly mistakes

Another reason why managers are reluctant to delegate is the possibility that subordinates will cause a great deal of damage for which the manager will be held accountable. This is a valid excuse, but this risk can be reduced through training and initial close supervision. Delegation is not just simply a matter of handing over and saying: "Carry on!" That would be foolish. The manager must make sure that the subordinate is competent, but after that he must take the risk of trusting the subordinate. It is a risk – but all businessmen understand that risk is the basis for success.

> Many a growing business has failed because the entrepreneur was unwilling to delegate authority to other managers.
> Initially the business is small enough for the owner to manage by himself, but as it becomes more successful and starts expanding, it flounders because of the top man's inability (or unwillingness) to manage managers rather than manage workers.

Reluctance to let go

Another barrier to delegating is when the manager sees himself as the expert or the only one with a sense of responsibility. He is always saying: "If I do it myself, I know it will be done right." That is also a valid argument, but it means that the manager ends up doing almost everything himself.

> In my study I have a cartoon of a very harassed manager who is saying to himself:
> "I do everything around here" – because –
> "My staff don't know enough" – because –
> "I don't do enough training" – because –
> "I don't have the time" – because –
> "I do everything around here."
> That is known as a vicious circle!

At another South African building society the general manager insisted that all mortgage bonds granted to staff members (under a fringe benefit scheme) had to be approved by him personally, despite the fact that hundreds of mortgage bonds were approved by the bonds department each year. He was often away on business trips and it caused a great deal of delay and frustration among his subordinates.

When I challenged him as to why he had to approve those bonds personally, he told me that, despite several of the middle managers scrutinising the applications, he often found some negative aspect that they had overlooked.

"You must be looking for things that they don't look for," I suggested.

"That's right," he said, glad that he could justify his actions.

"Why don't you tell them what those things are?" I suggested, "then you won't have to do it all yourself."

He didn't have an answer.

> The regional manager of a timber company had tried for two years to persuade his foresters to delegate responsibility to their subordinates. It was, however, difficult since the foresters continued to hang on to the responsibility themselves and continually give instructions to their labourers.

> The regional manager then took a drastic step. He suggested to two chainsaw operators that they should resign from the company and work as independent contractors. They should employ and pay their own subordinates, and pay for all expenses (including rental of the chainsaw). They would then be remunerated for the volume of timber that they harvest.
>
> A week after the two chainsaw operators started as contractors, the other chainsaw operators wanted to go on to the same basis, and so thirty contractor teams were appointed. Three supervisors were also appointed as independent "agents", and they were remunerated for the quality of the work produced by their group of ten contractors.
>
> The results were very impressive. Within the first two months the company's harvesting costs came down by 30 per cent despite the fact that everybody was earning more. The productivity rose from 2,2 tons per man-day to 3,7 tons per man-day. Absenteeism was almost zero, while the fuel consumption and repair costs also came down considerably. The contractors also resigned as members of the trade union.
>
> When I asked one of the contractors why he was now working so hard, he said it was because of the money he could now earn. When I pointed out to him that under the previous bonus system he could have earned just as much, he replied: "Yes, but now I am my own boss!"

I don't believe that appointing workers as independent contractors is the only way to motivate them. It can be done just as effectively while they are still employed by the company, but then managers must delegate real responsibility – and they must treat subordinates as if they are "their own boss".

Feeling threatened

Some managers may feel that their subordinates will lose respect for them if they can perform a task better than the manager can. They feel that they have to "justify" their managerial position by outperforming their subordinates.

I wonder where the idea that a manager should be more competent than his subordinates came from? Nobody questions the fact that a world-class boxer's manager cannot box as well as his subordinate. He doesn't have to; he is there to manage, not to box.

A manager does not have to compete with his subordinates to prove himself. He is there to manage, not to do the work. I believe it was Sir Harry Oppenheimer who said that the key to successful leadership was to "pick competent subordinates and let them get on with the job". That does not mean that any good leader can manage any organisation. A manager must have sufficient knowledge and technical insight to be able to evaluate the performance of his subordinates, but he does not have to do the work as well as they can.

Enjoyment of "technical" work

Managers are also reluctant to delegate because they enjoy "getting involved". Many sales managers seem to enjoy customer contact far more than being the man behind the scenes encouraging his sales staff. Many an engineer who is in a management position still enjoys "getting his hands dirty" rather than "getting results through people". There are numerous accountants who still enjoy writing up the books. Why is this so?

Perhaps one of the reasons is that it gives them a feeling of competence or success. It is something that they can do well – that's why they were promoted in the first place – and it is difficult for any person to accept the fact that the very thing that led to his promotion (his technical expertise) is the wrong thing to do now that he is in a managerial position.

> One of the trends over the last decade or so has been the appointment of "non-experts" to top management positions of large corporations. Some of the large insurance companies in South Africa, for example, have brought in non-actuaries from the outside.
>
> These men have been able to give the organisation a broad management perspective without getting involved in the technical details.

Perhaps another reason why managers enjoy technical work is that it keeps them busy and doesn't require much thinking. As a vegetable farmer said to me: "I enjoy sitting in the shed with my workers knocking nails into tomato boxes." At least he has something to show for his efforts, but in the process he is neglecting his proactive management tasks.

Delegating is a time-consuming process

Delegation requires training and coaching – and that takes time. So often managers say: "I'll delegate next time when we are not under so much pressure," but the pressure only increases.

> That is like the woodcutter who has no time to sharpen his axe because he is too busy chopping down trees.

Delegation does take time because there are four basic steps that have to be followed:
Step 1 is telling the subordinate *what* a certain responsibility implies and *how* to deal with it. Then the manager must do it himself while the subordinate just watches. In the process the manager must tell him *why* it has to be done.

Why the "why"? If all things run smoothly, then the "what" and the "how" may be sufficient, but if a subordinate does not understand the "why", he will not be able to use his discretion to take corrective action when things go wrong.

Step 2 is presenting the subordinate with the problem and he must tell the manager what he would do. The manager asks questions and comments on his approach.

This is giving the subordinate some theoretical training and cannot be skipped – particularly not with black subordinates, whose culture prevents them from saying "no" when asked if they understand. They must describe their proposed action in their own words.

Step 3 is giving the subordinate the actual task or situation to deal with while the manager keeps a close watch on him and gives him appropriate feedback.

This step may take some time, depending on the complexity of the task and the competence of the subordinate – but it cannot be short-circuited. A manager must satisfy himself that the subordinate is equipped to take on the responsibility.

Step 4 is assigning the responsibility to the subordinate as part of his job. The subordinate accepts full responsibility and all that is left for the manager to do is to agree on the goals and to monitor the results. This completes the delegation process.

Note that goal setting and monitoring of results cannot be delegated. That will always be part of a manager's job.

Conclusion

Participation in decision making not only stimulates creativity, but also exposes a subordinate to solving problems that he is not yet experienced enough to deal with on his own. Delegation of responsibility goes a step further. It allows a subordinate to solve problems on his own. Effective leadership is to use both approaches – for it is the only way a manager can give a subordinate the opportunity to prove himself.

15 MANAGEMENT CONTROLS

The role of management controls

The third expectation of a subordinate is to let him know how he's doing – whether it's good or bad. To be in a position to do that a manager has to have effective management controls. The greatest reason for failure in the implementation of a management-by-end-result approach is the failure to install an effective management control system.

> Every now and then I meet managers who tell me that after my seminar they got off to a great start, but that with time the whole thing slowly faded away.
> In almost all the cases they failed to introduce an official measuring system.

I wish I could dramatise the importance of sound management controls, but I don't know how to. The whole management approach can be compared with building a motor car. *Setting objectives* is like building the chassis. Everything rests on it, but after it has been built we don't need to give it much attention. *Delegating* can be compared with the engine. The more we delegate, the greater the capacity that we generate. We certainly need to give more attention to delegation (the engine) than to goal setting (the chassis). But the aspect of the motor car that gets the most attention is the fuel. We have to put that in regularly. *Management controls* provide the "fuel" that keeps the whole system going, because what you measure is what you get.

The purpose of management controls

A management control system serves two major purposes. Firstly, it must *determine whether the work of a subordinate meets the required standard.*

Every manager understands the need for making sure that the work of his subordinates is done correctly and we have no problem with this concept.

Very few managers, however, seem to bother about the second purpose of management controls, and that is to *keep a record of the performance of individual subordinates*. Most managers will go to great lengths to check that the work is up to standard (the first purpose), but very few managers bother to keep a systematic record of performance (the second purpose). The result is that they are seldom in a position to meet that very important expectation of a subordinate, namely, to let him know how he's doing. Nor do they have an accurate and objective record on which to base the reward system.

> Most managers have no difficulty in identifying the subordinates who perform exceptionally well or the subordinates who are performing poorly.
>
> It's the in-betweens that we find difficult to assess accurately when we have no performance records.

When it comes to exercising management control, most managers seem to use one of two basic approaches. They either exercise it through the *inspection of activities* or through the *measurement of end results*.

Inspection of activities

Method

In this approach the manager simply supervises the activities of his subordinates while they work. (In Afrikaans such a person is referred to as a "passer en draaier" – "Hy pas die werkers op terwyl hy 'n zol draai.") We see a great deal of this with municipal workers digging up a road or cutting down a tree. There is usually somebody standing (or sitting) to make sure that they keep busy. This type of "snoopervision" is one version of Inspection of Activities.

A more common version is for a manager to check all the work of his subordinates to see if it is "all right". Note that he does not measure any standard of performance or keep any record of achievement. He just wants to be sure that it is "okay".

> Typical examples of this approach are managers going over all written work produced by their subordinates to check for any mistakes (although they never keep record of the number of mistakes found); supervisors seeing that physical work like gardening is "acceptable" (but never giving the gardener a performance rating, let alone keeping a record); foremen inspecting samples of products to check for any defects (without keeping record of the number of items that had to be reworked).

The focus of Inspection of Activities is on the first purpose of management controls only – to ensure that the work of a subordinate meets the required standard. The second purpose is completely ignored. There are, however, some advantages to this type of control.

Advantages

The first advantage is that the manager knows exactly how the work is progressing. He has his finger on the pulse at all times. Secondly, mistakes can be prevented or corrected quickly before any serious damage is done. Finally, it does keep subordinates moving if they know that the boss is watching or continually checking up on them. These are probably the major reasons why so many managers practise Inspection of Activities.

Disadvantages

The biggest disadvantage is that this type of control is extremely time-consuming – usually at the expense of the proactive management tasks that are neglected in the process.

> A farmer in the Eastern Transvaal who knew of no other method of control expressed his frustration by saying: "I'm not a manager. I'm only a white induna, because all day long I do nothing but stand here and watch my workers. I never have time for things like financial planning, farm development, experimenting with new ideas, or anything like that."
> However, this farmer changed his entire management process around and achieved amazing success in the motivation of his workers (Mol 1984).

Another disadvantage is that subordinates tend to switch off mentally since the boss is always on hand to solve any problems. It takes a tremendous amount of self-discipline for a manager not to give a solution whenever a subordinate asks him: "What do I do now?" but rather to encourage him to come up with the answer himself.

The third disadvantage is that subordinates tend to be productive only while the boss is watching.

> A housewife in Pretoria had a gardener who kept the garden in immaculate condition and she seldom had to tell him what to do.
> One day she went out to where he was neatening the edge of a flower bed with a spade. His slow pace of work annoyed her intensely, so she grabbed the spade out of his hands and worked furiously for a minute or so. "That's how you must work," she said, as she handed the spade back to him.
> However, he was one of those workers who talk back: "Madam, if I have to demonstrate how to work for one minute, I can also work that fast."
> She was about to fire him for his insolence when it struck her that she had assessed him on his activity, not on his end result. "Well, all right, carry on," she said rather awkwardly as she beat a hasty retreat.
> What if he had not spoken out? He would have increased his work pace until she disappeared and then he would have returned to his old pace – but with two pains: one in his heart for the unreasonableness of it all and the other in his neck – to keep looking out for her over his shoulder while working.

Usage

Despite all its disadvantages, there is a use for the Inspection of Activities approach. The first is with subordinates who are still in the process of learning. As discussed in the previous chapter, it would be foolhardy for a manager to delegate responsibility without making quite sure that the subordinate is capable of handling the job on his own. This requires training *and* initial close supervision: in other words, Inspection of Activities.

The second situation where Inspection of Activities is warranted is where a subordinate does not achieve the desired results. Then the manager has to investigate what the subordinate is actually doing that is causing his poor performance – but apart from these two situations, the most effective approach to controlling the work of subordinates is through the measurement of the end result.

Measurement of end results

Method

This approach involves the regular gathering of quantitative work results that have been identified as the objectives for that particular position. For example, controlling the work performance of the production supervisor (discussed in chapter 13) would mean that his immediate superior would have to obtain information on the units produced, the reject rate, the scrap rate, the breakdown hours, etc.

This information must then be recorded systematically on a control sheet or in a control book for each job incumbent. It will require more than one sheet depending on how frequently the information is obtained. There may, for example, be a daily performance record for some outputs, while other data is obtained on a weekly, monthly or even a quarterly basis.

In the case of the production supervisor all the data could be collected on a daily basis. This would require a control sheet for each month with a place to record the daily performance for each yardstick, as well as a monthly average. This monthly average would then be transferred to a control sheet that shows the performance for each month of the year, as well as the annual average.

Whatever the system, it is essential that performance results be recorded systematically. In positions where there are some daily measurements and some monthly measurements, the daily average should be transferred to the month sheet, which should also have room for monthly figures that are recorded for the first time.

In other words, the control sheets should be linked to a time period (day, week, month, quarter) where the averages of the shorter periods are transferred to the control sheets of the next time period, until it finally culminates in an annual performance record.

The results (at the time that they become known) are then compared with the goals. Good performance is reinforced with a compliment and poor performance is corrected. Note that poor performance does not mean every time the daily or weekly results are below par. Room must be allowed for fluctuations in performance. It is only when a major problem is identified or a definite trend of poor results is highlighted over a period of time that the manager needs to take corrective action.

> It is very important to distinguish between *recording* performance and *evaluating* performance. Management controls are primarily for the purpose of recording information. How that information is interpreted to evaluate the employee concerned will always require sound management judgment.
>
> The biggest danger in evaluating the performance of an employee is that management will look only at the final figure and not take into account a number of other aspects that might have affected the final result.
>
> Management may also be tempted to compare the global performance figure of one employee with those of another employee, without taking into account the unique circumstances of each individual. In this way a subordinate could be condemned unfairly.
>
> If the information produced by the management control system is used as a whipping stick, it will do more harm than not measuring performance at all.

The Measurement of End Results approach achieves both purposes of control. It provides the manager with information on the standard of work that his subordinates are producing, and it also provides him with a record of performance.

Advantages

These are considerable. In the first place it saves the manager a great deal of time, since he does not have to spend all his time checking up on his subordinates.

> A chicken company near East London found that after they switched over from Inspection of Activities to Measurement of End Results, a farm manager was able to cope comfortably with twice the number of chicken houses per farm.

> Whereas before the farm manager spent a great deal of his time in the chicken houses telling the workers what to do, he now only had to go to each house once a day to measure the results in four performance areas.
> These results were then recorded on two copies of the control sheet – one for the office and one for the chicken house itself.
> In a relatively short period of time the profits soared.

Another advantage is that performance can be evaluated objectively rather than relying on general impressions. Performance appraisal is a dreaded exercise for some managers. They don't have sufficient data on which to base an accurate assessment and, in order not to upset any of their subordinates, they tend to rate most of them as "above average". Very few employees will argue with that assessment, but it is doubtful whether it will lead to any improvement in performance.

When the performance appraisal is based on measured end results, the assessment can be far more objective. Instead of trying to defend his rating to a subordinate, the manager can devote his time to discussing ways and means to improve the results in the future.

Perhaps the greatest advantage is the fact that subordinates know exactly what they are measured on. This encourages them to start exercising control themselves and to use their initiative in taking corrective action before the manager is even aware of any deviation.

> The concept of self-control is a very important one. The control system must be designed in such a way that the job incumbent is the first to be informed of the work results.

Disadvantages

Despite the many advantages, there are some disadvantages to the Measurement of End Results approach. The first is that mistakes may come to the attention of the manager too late – particularly where the data is recorded weekly or monthly.

This drawback can be eliminated to some extent through periodic spot checks by the manager, or through the use of the "confessional system" where subordinates are encouraged to report all problems immediately.

> The manager of the financial division in a large South African corporation told his sixty-odd staff that if they made a mistake of any kind (even if it was forgetting to attend to an important matter) and they reported it to their immediate superior, it would not be kept on record or held against them in any way. If, however, the mistake was picked up by management, it *would* be counted against them.
>
> This prompted subordinates to report problems immediately – and the manager's chance of being caught by surprise was reduced considerably.

So often subordinates are reluctant to report any problems for fear of being reprimanded. They reason that if the boss finds out they will be reprimanded anyway, but he might not find out. It's always in their favour not to say anything. The "confessional system" creates just the opposite attitude.

> There are some management authors who advocate a Control by Exception approach, where a manager is informed only of serious deviations.
>
> The "confessional system" is a form of Control by Exception, but it cannot be used in isolation, for then the manager would only know if things went wrong. That would accomplish the first purpose of management control but certainly not the second.

The second disadvantage of measuring only the end results is the bother of having to design a comprehensive control data system – especially if the data is collected at varying time intervals. So many managers put off the design of such a control sheet until later when they will "have more time". In the end, nothing comes of it.

To design all the different control sheets for each position *is* a bother. It takes time and lots of experimentation – yet the results are well worth the effort.

Lastly, Measurement of End Results requires a great deal of self-discipline on the part of the manager to stay out of the subordinate's way as long as he is achieving his objectives.

> The same Pretoria housewife I have already mentioned has been very successful in motivating her gardener by going through the garden with him each Saturday morning and giving him a rating on the attractiveness of the garden.
> One morning, however, she found him fast asleep under a tree. Her first inclination was to kick him, but on second thoughts she decided to wait until Saturday's evaluation.
> That Saturday she could find nothing wrong and she had to give him a very high rating.

The focus must be on the end result and not on how busy the worker is. If the garden is beautiful (the end result), the gardener should be allowed to sleep. Of course, if he sleeps most of the time and still produces a beautiful garden, he needs a bigger garden, or he should be given additional responsibilities.

Usage

When should the Measurement of End Results approach be used? It is the *only* method to control the work of competent subordinates. There is no managerial justification for constantly supervising work activity.

With less competent or inexperienced workers it should also be used – but in conjunction with the Inspection of Activities approach. As the subordinate achieves the end results, the manager can gradually withdraw this inspection until the subordinate is measured only on end results.

> The regional manager of a timber company has just gone through the exercise of identifying the performance areas and yardsticks for his district managers. The monthly control sheet comprises no more than one page of figures, where previously up to twenty pages of figures were looked at.
> Two of the district managers are, however, fairly new in the position, and the regional manager checks and discusses figures for

their districts in much more detail, using it as an opportunity to train the district managers in the finer points.

He plans to use this dual system of control until such time as each district manager has shown both the ability and the confidence to be left on his own.

That's good management.

Conclusion

I have no doubt that the measuring system in an organisation is one of the most powerful determinants of management behaviour. Accountants need to be especially sensitive to this fact when designing the management information system of a company. So often accountants love to collect all kinds of data and to play around with the figures without realising the impact it has on organisational behaviour. They need to remember that they only count the beans – they don't produce them.

Conflict between the accounting division and other divisions in the company is not uncommon for this very reason. Accountants can be a tremendous asset in helping to design the right kind of control system, but they can also be a terrible hindrance.

16 DEALING WITH A NON-PERFORMER

Options

It's all very well to praise the good performer and encourage him to continue with his success pattern, but what about the underachiever? How does a manager deal with a subordinate who is not meeting the required standard? What can he say to motivate him to improve his performance? For many managers this is a rather unpleasant task – one that they would rather avoid.

> A new manager was appointed to a retail store where the assistant manager had worked for almost 25 years. This assistant manager, however, did not have the ability (or the inclination) to take on the full management responsibility of the store.
> At the same time he was not prepared to accept the authority of the relatively inexperienced manager who had been appointed over him. He challenged him continually, openly refused to obey orders in front of the other employees, and resisted all attempts to establish a good working relationship.
> The store manager did not have the authority to fire the assistant manager, so he went to the regional manager and told him that it was impossible to work with the assistant manager since his authority was being seriously undermined.
> The regional manager simply told him that they must sort it out themselves.

This regional manager was obviously avoiding the unpleasantness of the situation and probably hoping that the problem would resolve itself. But there is little doubt that he is about to lose the store manager (and subsequent successors) if he does not take some action.

Some managers choose a different option. They don't say anything to the underachiever himself, but they punish him in some way or other, for example, by giving him a poor salary increase at the end of the year or even by firing him on some flimsy excuse. Others take the first opportunity to solve the problem by recommending that he be transferred to another part of the company. But at no stage will they discuss the problem openly with the subordinate.

> A senior researcher at a scientific institute near Pretoria had such poor interpersonal relations with his staff, that he was on the point of being fired. As a last resort he was sent to one of my management seminars in the hope that it would make him realise where he was going wrong.
> Some weeks later a secretary phoned me for an appointment saying that the researcher wanted to discuss his problems with me. At that stage I was unaware of his problems with his staff.
> His boss simply told him that an appointment had been made for him: "Dr Mol would like to discuss certain things with you." You can imagine the surprise when we found that neither of us knew what it was all about.
> He did tell me, though, that he clashed with two people in his department, and that his boss had spoken to him about it, but that the three of them had never been called in to the office together to discuss the matter openly.
> His boss was obviously avoiding a confrontation.

It is obvious that these options are not very effective and the problem will only deteriorate. For this reason some managers get "tough" with the non-performers by scolding them and calling them all kinds of names. By blowing his top and yelling at his staff the manager may relieve some of his pent-up frustrations, but it is unlikely that the worker's performance will improve for very long. Next time the manager will have to shout a little louder to get the same response. At the same time it will create a great deal of resentment that may motivate the subordinate to get back at the manager in some way or other.

Attack leads to defence

Whenever a person is criticised or has his mistakes pointed out to him, he is being attacked. No matter how correct the manager may be, or how accurate his facts are, or how politely he states his case, it is still an attack – and a person who is attacked will defend himself, usually in one of three ways.

Counterattack

This implies that when the manager points out the shortcomings in the performance of the subordinate, the subordinate becomes very aggressive. He will criticise the company and/or the manager, blaming them for his poor performance. This will put the manager on the defensive and lead to a rather unpleasant argument.

> Many married couples use the technique of counterattack. For example, when a wife criticises her husband for leaving mud on her new carpet, he defends himself by criticising her appearance and in no time she forgets all about the mud.
> This may be a very effective form of defence, but it doesn't do much for the marriage relationship.

When a subordinate counterattacks, a manager sometimes backs down because he cannot match the subordinate in a battle of words. Perhaps he doesn't want to lose the subordinate because he is a key employee. In either case the subordinate has won and there will certainly be no change in his performance. In the process the manager has lost considerable authority. No wonder managers are reluctant to confront poor performers.

On the other hand, the manager may retaliate by using his authority, either firing the subordinate or threatening to fire him if he doesn't improve. In both cases the manager has failed to motivate the worker to improve his work performance.

"Yessir!"

Some subordinates will not talk back to the manager when he points out their shortcomings. They simply say: "Yes, Sir, no, Sir, very well, Sir." When the manager walks away they say: "I'll get you back, Sir."

> Some years ago a friend of mine worked at a motorcar factory in the Eastern Cape. One particular day they were confronted with a luxury car that had been returned by the owner because of an irritating rattle. The dealer had tried in vain to trace the cause.

> In the factory they tried almost everything, but without success – until they finally took the car apart piece by piece, and found a screwdriver in one of the upright struts. A piece of paper was attached to the screwdriver with an elastic band, and written on it were the words: "So you found it at last."
> Further investigation revealed that the screwdriver had belonged to a worker who had been dismissed a few weeks earlier. That was his way of defending himself.
> My friend estimated that it must have cost the company close on R100 000.
> A very expensive dismissal!

I am of the opinion that many workers in South Africa use this form of defence when they are reprimanded by a manager. They don't talk back; they just say: "Yessir." But some time later there is an "accident" or some tools go missing, or some other form of sabotage takes place.

People who are attacked will always defend themselves, and the "Yessir" method is the most difficult to deal with since management is not even aware of it. They don't link the "sabotage" with the scolding they dished out a few days earlier.

Excuses

Some subordinates will defend themselves by coming up with all kinds of excuses as to why the poor performance was not really their fault. They either blame circumstances, or they blame other people, but they will always try to convince the manager that they had no control over what happened.

What do most managers do when subordinates make excuses for poor performance? The initial reaction is usually to "prove" to the subordinate that the excuse is not valid. The subordinate will then try to prove that the excuse *is* valid – and now they are in a competition that will produce a winner and a loser.

Research has shown that a subordinate will persist even more in the wrong behaviour after the reprimand than before, because if he changes, it will be as good as admitting: "The boss has won and I have lost." Nobody wants to lose and a win/lose situation will actually prevent any change in behaviour.

> My experience as marriage counsellor suggests that the greatest source of conflict between husband and wife is the win/lose situation that they so often find themselves in.
>
> One couple experienced major conflict over the time the husband came home each evening. He often had a beer in the pub after work and the more his wife nagged him to come home early, the later he came. Eventually she threatened to give his dinner to the dog if he wasn't home by seven o'clock. Of course, he didn't come home before seven and the dog thought it was Christmas.
>
> Privately, however, he told me that he would like to come home early to spend some time with his kids but that he was scared that she would greet him with a smirk on her face, indicating that she had finally won and he had lost.
>
> She had prevented the very thing she wanted, because she had created a win/lose situation with her attack.

It is imperative that managers should find a way of dealing with an underachiever without getting caught in the win/lose trap.

The objective

At the outset it is important to realise that the purpose of dealing with a non-performer is *not* to point out the mistakes that he has made in the past, but to bring about changes in his future actions. A manager can do nothing about the past, and to harp on the mistakes, or to place the blame on the subordinate, only leads to defensiveness on the part of the individual concerned.

Not only must the focus be on the future; it must be on changing the subordinate's future *behaviour* rather than on changing his attitude. It is a mistaken belief that attitude leads to behaviour. The opposite is more likely: behaviour leads to attitude.

> A manager who had attended one of my management seminars was determined to prove me wrong. The only way he could do this was to try out the approach I had advocated; so he picked on his "worst" employee.

If we apply these management principles to a good worker it is understandable that he will perform well, but when a poor worker starts achieving good results it is doubly impressive. That is exactly what happened in this case, and the manager is now a keen human resource manager.

He left the seminar with the wrong attitude, but he did the right things. The result was a major change in his attitude stemming from a change in his behaviour.

Steps in dealing with a non-performer

Step 1: Present the problem factually and offer your help in finding a solution

"John, I am concerned at the high number of rejects we have had this month. What can I do to help you?"

"Frank, the absenteeism rate in your department is quite high. Is there anything I can do to help you?"

"Susan, we have had several customer complaints about incorrect invoicing. How can I help you to overcome that problem?"

What message does a manager convey when he offers his help to an underachiever? He is saying: "I am on your side." This approach is referred to as "we versus the problem" rather than "you versus me". "You versus me" only leads to a win/lose situation. Offering help to a subordinate, however, takes the sting out of a perceived attack.

When I was at school fights were often scheduled "behind the woodwork room" at break time. This was very exciting, especially for the spectators. But most of us outgrow those childish things – those who don't go to parliament.

There we see highly-paid adults playing "you versus me" games like a bunch of kids. In my opinion most politicians are not really interested in solving the country's problems – they are only interested in defeating their political opponents. Their childishness is clearly evidenced by the silly posters they put up at election time.

The opposition will almost always criticise the government's proposed legislation – no matter how good it may be – and the government will almost always reject the opposition's amendments, regardless of merit. What matters to them is who is going to win – not what is best for the country.

Meanwhile the country is governed by the civil servants who seem to go ahead merrily, regardless of what the politicians say. Perhaps that is why South Africa has one of the largest civil services in the Western world.

The "we versus the problem" approach is an extremely useful concept in all areas of conflict. If opposing but interdependent parties would only get on the same side, there is no problem that cannot be solved. As long as the "you versus me" approach is maintained, there is no problem that is solvable.

Time and again I have seen husbands and wives destroying one another because they see each other as opponents. "I'm right, you're wrong" is at the root of all interpersonal conflict. It is only when they get to the stage where they say: "We're both right – how can we solve the problem?" that a solution is possible. In my book *Let's both win* (1981) I deal with this topic in more detail.

Step 2: Accept his excuses without argument and bring him back to the solution

"Yes, I can understand why you did that. What can we do to solve it?"

"I can see why you reacted the way you did, but what can we do to prevent the problem recurring?"

"Yes, I can understand why you were prevented from taking effective action. What can we do to overcome those obstacles?"

Even though a manager offers his help, the subordinate may still see it as an attack and offer his excuses. But how long can a subordinate continue to defend himself when the manager accepts his excuses (even if he doesn't think that they are valid) and focuses on a solution?

The key to dealing with a non-performer is to attack the *problem* and not the person. Even if it is clear that the subordinate is at fault, it serves no purpose to attack him. It will only put him on the defensive. Rather attack the problem.

> This is an important principle when it comes to disciplining children. The harmful side of discipline is when parents attack the child by calling him all kinds of names and labelling him "naughty", "lazy", "stupid", etc.
>
> When I spanked my kids when they were small, I would say something like: "Come here, my boy. What you have done does not suit a super little kid like you," and then I would spank him.
>
> In the process I attacked his behaviour, not his character. This topic is covered in detail in my book *Parenting isn't child's play* (1984).

Step 3: Involve him in finding a solution and agree on a plan of action

It is essential that the subordinate should come up with the answer himself. As mentioned in chapter 10, when a subordinate proposes a solution, he has made an emotional investment. It's his judgment that is at stake, and he will be far more committed to the solution than when it comes from the manager.

Of course, if he does not know what the answer is, the manager needs to guide him by asking some leading questions, and ultimately the manager may have no choice but to tell him what to do. This may not be too serious if the subordinate is still in the process of learning, but if we are dealing with an experienced subordinate it may be an indication that he is not equipped to hold that position.

> What happens if a subordinate proposes a solution that is not acceptable to the manager? He may, for example, ask for additional staff to overcome the delays in his section, or he may propose the purchase of new or additional equipment.

> There can obviously be no hard and fast rules as to what the manager should do. However, he must always give the subordinate an honest answer if his request cannot be granted. The worst thing a manager can do is to tell the subordinate that he'll think about it and then hope that with time the subordinate will forget about it. If the manager turns down the subordinate's request, but with good reasons, he may not like it, but he will probably accept it. The damage is done when a manager tries to pull the wool over his subordinate's eyes by stalling the answer.

Dealing with a non-performer must result in a *plan of action* in terms of what the subordinate will do and, if applicable, what the manager will do to solve the problem. Remember that the manager's task is to help him, not condemn him.

This plan of action must be in terms of specific activities that will be carried out in the next few days or weeks. The more specific the plan, the greater the likelihood that the subordinate will be successful in solving the problem or overcoming his poor performance. Merely giving him a pep talk in the hope that it will change his attitude is usually futile.

Step 4: Agree on a short-term goal and set a review date

The final step is to agree on a specific goal that is to be achieved in the next week or month. As discussed in chapter 13, it must be a measurable goal that is within the subordinate's reach.

This goal (and perhaps the action plan as well) must be put in writing. It does not have to be a formal letter – it can even be written on the back of a cigarette box – as long as both manager and subordinate have a copy. A written agreement carries much more weight and it also prevents misunderstandings where a subordinate might say later: "Oh, but I thought you meant . . . "

Finally, the manager must make quite sure that he assesses the performance on the review date; otherwise the subordinate will get the impression that the boss wasn't really serious about the whole matter.

> More management actions have come to grief for lack of follow-up measurement than any other reason.

Principles

The following principles should be borne in mind:
- Never attack a subordinate by pointing out his shortcomings or by implying that he is to blame for the poor performance.
- The manager is there to help the subordinate, not condemn him. This is a basic expectation of every subordinate.
- Focus on finding a solution, and not on finding fault: attack the problem, not the person.
- If the subordinate improves, reinforce the improvement with positive feedback and set new goals with him.

What happens if the subordinate does not improve sufficiently or there is no significant change in his behaviour? Some managers say that the subordinate must then be fired (or given a written warning, depending on the laid-down procedures), but it would be hard to justify penalising an employee after only one discussion – unless of course he has committed a very serious offence.

If a subordinate does not improve, the correct approach is to go back to step 1. "George, we agreed that by today you would have caught up on your backlog by at least 50 per cent. You are still in the same position as two weeks ago. What can we do to solve this problem?" The same procedure is followed resulting in a specific action plan and new short-term goals.

If there is still no improvement, I suggest that you go through the whole process again – but with an added warning. "Christine, I want you to be successful in this job, and I will help you all I can. But if you cannot meet the required standard, I will have no choice but to penalise you or replace you. I cannot lower my standards."

> Obviously a manager must never hold out consequences to a subordinate that he is not in a position to carry out. If his bluff is called, his authority will be seriously undermined.
> It also goes without saying that, if the company has a disciplinary code, it must be adhered to at all times.

My management philosophy

The warning set out above is not intended as a threat. It is an honest attempt to help the subordinate to be successful in his job. There is still the element of encouragement and support. But it does reflect the management philosophy that I have presented throughout this book, namely to be *tough*.

My experience with South African managers is that they are much too lenient when it comes to dealing with subordinates – especially the un-skilled and semi-skilled work-force. It's time that managers became *hard* in their management of subordinates.

☐ Hard on *standards*
☐ Soft on *people*

Hard on standards implies that a manager is not prepared to put up with mediocre work performance. He insists on excellence and is prepared to go out of his way to help his subordinates to achieve it. At the same time he is soft on people – he always treats subordinates with dignity and respect.

Most traditional managers are just the other way around. They are soft on standards and hard on people. If the worker performs an average job, the manager is inclined to accept it saying: "What else can one expect." But when the subordinate makes a mistake, the traditional manager jumps on him, scolding him and telling him how useless he is.

The human relations manager is inclined to be soft on standards and soft on people, with the result that he seldom gets good performance and his subordinates are inclined to take advantage of him.

A factory manager had one of his charge hands arriving late for work fairly frequently. He called him in and asked what he could do to help him solve this problem. The charge hand assured him that it wouldn't happen again, but it did.

Again the manager called him in and explained that he was one of the senior workers in the factory and that his poor example was having a negative effect on the rest of the work-force.

His punctuality improved for a short while and then reverted to the same pattern. This time the manager added a warning, telling him that he was a good charge hand and that he didn't want to lose him, but that he would have no choice but to dismiss him if his punctuality did not improve.

The charge hand probably didn't believe that the manager would take such drastic action because some weeks later he was again arriving late two or three times a week.

When the manager quietly called him in and gave him his notice, the subordinate got a fright and begged to be given another chance.

> However, the manager replied: "I'm sorry, I have already given you two chances. I cannot lower my standards."

That factory manager told me later that he was sorry to have let a good charge hand go, but he was pleased with the way he had handled it. He had been tough on his standards but soft on the individual. He had not humiliated the man; nor had he degraded himself.

> When a manager curses and yells at subordinates, he is actually lowering himself to the point where not only his staff lose respect for him, but he loses respect for himself.

The sad part is that scolding subordinates doesn't lead to any improvement in their performance; it only lowers their own self-image. They begin to see themselves as useless, no-good so-and-so's, and will then behave that way.

Conclusion

Every manager has the choice of helping his subordinates to improve their performance or condemning them for their incompetence. They will become whatever he thinks of them. The more he seeks to praise and encourage them, the more confident they will become. The more he runs them down, the worse they will become.

17 REWARDS THAT MOTIVATE

What is a reward?

The last expectation that subordinates have of their managers is to be rewarded for their contribution. Companies have sought to reward their employees in a multitude of different ways – anything from a photograph on the noticeboard as "Worker of the Month" to a trip around the world with all expenses paid. But when is a reward a reward? How large must it be before it will have a motivating effect on the individual concerned? Will all subordinates value a reward to the same extent?

The key that makes a reward rewarding is *recognition*. It is not so much the nature of the reward that matters or the size of it, but that it was given specifically in recognition of good performance.

> It never ceases to amaze me that most employees find it difficult to recall what their salary increase was two years ago – especially if it was an adjustment given to everybody in the company, even a large one.
>
> Yet they will remember in detail what the MD said ten years ago when he made a special point of complimenting them on a job well done.

As soon as the company gives the employee something that he considers to be his *right*, it has lost its motivational value. That is why it is not a healthy practice to promise subordinates some kind of benefit if they perform well. A potential reward then becomes a right – as is the case with incentive schemes.

Psychological rewards

There are three types of reward that a manager has at his disposal and, for want of a better word, I have called the first type *psychological rewards*.

The first psychological reward is a *compliment for a job well done*. When we give somebody a sincere compliment, it creates a very strong desire to maintain, if not improve on, the standard. This was discussed in detail in chapter 11 and need not be repeated here, but it remains the most powerful motivator there is. It must be remembered that a compliment must be given in the light of the subordinate's ability. Don't wait until he can do a task as well as you can – praise him if it is an achievement for him.

> We do this naturally with small children. I used to praise my four-year-old daughter for eating so nicely with her mouth closed, but I couldn't give that compliment to my wife. Not that she eats with her mouth open, but it isn't an achievement for her.

One warning: avoid any form of flattery or manipulation. The compliment must be genuine recognition; otherwise it will do more harm than good. Years ago I worked for somebody who had only recently been promoted to personnel manager, having spent many years in the company as sales manager. From the very first day he told me what a high regard he had for me. He called me doctor and professor (long before I was) and told me that since I was an expert in the field of manpower management, he would have to lean heavily on me.

Initially I enjoyed all this praise, but as time went on I realised that, although he kept telling me how terrific I was, he hardly ever consulted me or even asked my opinion. In the eighteen months that I worked for him he delegated one task to me – because he was out of town and unable to do it himself.

It wasn't long before all his nice words turned sour, and I began to resent them because I knew that they were not sincere. He was just trying to flatter me in an attempt to keep me happy, but it backfired on him because shortly afterwards I handed in my resignation.

Psychological rewards should not be limited only to employees who achieve outstanding results. What about those who put in a good deal of extra effort? *A word of appreciation for work beyond the call of duty* is another powerful reward. It is amazing how much extra effort people are willing to put in if the boss will only say "thank you", which is just another form of saying: "I recognise your efforts."

> A manager told me that late one afternoon he gave his secretary an urgent report to type while he attended another meeting. When he returned to his office later that evening, the report was on his desk.
> Since he was going to be away for the next few days, he put a piece of paper in her typewriter and wrote her a little thank-you note.
> When he got back to office some days later, the first thing she said to him was: "Thank you for my note." He could see how much it had meant to her that she was not just being taken for granted.

The third type of psychological reward is to *involve the subordinate in decision making*. It may seem strange that this is classified as a reward, but asking a subordinate for his opinion is a strong form of recognition – as long as it is sincere.

I read in a management book that a manager should put an idea across to his subordinates in such a way that they will think it is their idea. That is out-and-out manipulation and the subordinates will perceive it as such very quickly. (It might work with your boss, but not with your subordinates.)

Be honest. If you have already made up your mind, tell your subordinates exactly what you want them to do. Don't play clever psychological games. But, if you value their judgment, ask them. It is an important form of recognition.

> Some years ago I was asked to address the Economic Advisory Committee of the President's Council on ways and means of improving South Africa's labour productivity.
> I don't think it helped much, but I felt honoured at the recognition that I was given through this.

These psychological rewards are by far the most meaningful for any human being, but they are not enough in themselves. They need to be complemented by more tangible rewards.

> In organisations where there is very little scope for giving individuals tangible rewards, e.g. the teaching profession, the psychological rewards may be the only ones available to the principal. They will, therefore, play an important role in the motivation of teachers.

Social rewards

Again for want of a better word, I have called the second type of reward *social rewards*. These include rewards like *time off* in recognition for the extra effort that the subordinate has put in. If some of your staff, for example, have worked many hours of overtime in order to meet a deadline, it would be very appropriate to say to them: "Thanks for all the hard work you chaps have put in. I don't want to see you in the office on Friday – enjoy a nice long weekend." The time "lost" in this way cannot compare with the time gained through increased motivation and a willingness to put in that extra effort next time.

One thing to be careful of is "time-for-time" compensation. If the employee can go home an hour earlier every time he works an hour longer, he will begin to see it as his right, and it will then lose all its motivational impact.

Having a drink or a meal with subordinates to celebrate the completion of a successful project is another form of social reward.

> A manufacturing company in Pretoria operates three daily shifts. The shift that has the highest daily production gets a special reward. Each member of the shift is given a softdrink.
>
> The reward may seem rather small, but it is very significant to the workers. The reward lies not in its actual value, but in the fact that it serves as a recognition of their achievement.

The possibilities are endless – trips, special gifts, etc. One farmer in the Orange Free State put all his workers on a bus and took them to Durban for a weekend in a hotel. However, he made one management mistake. He took *all* of them.

For a reward to serve as recognition it must differentiate between the good performers and the not-so-good performers. If not, it will be perceived as part of their conditions of employment. In other words, if rewards are not linked to performance, they will be seen as a right.

> The story is told that when Howard Hughes was still president of the Lockheed Aircraft Corporation, he decided one year to give every employee a turkey for Thanksgiving Day.
> So refrigerated trucks came to the work-place and, as the workers knocked off, each one was handed a turkey "with the compliments of Mr Hughes". This wonderful gesture was talked about for days afterwards.
> Two weeks before Thanksgiving Day the following year, however, the personnel manager came to Mr Hughes and told him that there were speculations in the factory as to whether they would get a turkey again; perhaps it was better not to disappoint them.
> He agreed rather reluctantly, and everyone got another turkey. But two days later the complaints came pouring in. One man's turkey was a little off, another one's turkey was smaller than his mate's, a third one had been sick and wanted to know where he could pick up his turkey, and so on.
> Management then decided that the following year they would give everyone a gift voucher so that they could buy their own turkey at the local supermarket. However, the supermarket manager told the employees that they were welcome to buy other groceries as well if they wanted to – and so the whole goodwill gesture was lost.
> That year the trade union renegotiated the labour contract and guess what was part of the new contract? A turkey for Thanksgiving Day.

A similar incident occurred at a large South African manufacturing concern near Pretoria. Management decided that when the factories closed for the December vacation they would give every worker a slap-up luncheon on the last day. This they did for two years, but then the union wanted every employee to get the cash equivalent instead. So management reluctantly agreed to put R15 extra in every worker's pay packet in lieu of the luncheon, even though they realised that the luncheon would contribute more towards a team spirit.

The next year the union insisted that since the price of food had gone up, they now wanted R18 extra in every pay packet. That cost the company a great deal of money, without any additional motivation, simply because the "reward" was not linked to performance.

Fringe benefits like these are quite common. Most companies give their employees an annual bonus, often in the form of a double pay cheque. This is certainly not wrong – as long as management understands that it will have no effect on the motivation of their employees.

Financial rewards

The third type of reward, and probably the most common one, is a *financial reward*. It is important to understand the difference between remuneration and reward. *Remuneration* is the agreed payment that an employee can claim as his "right". This does not motivate employees – it only moves them. *Reward*, on the other hand, is payment given over and above the manager's obligation – and that motivates employees.

This means that most incentive schemes are nothing but forms of remuneration. A performance bonus, for example, does not motivate production workers; it moves them. Many factory foremen have made the mistake of thinking that the performance bonus provides the necessary driving force for their workers, and have, therefore, neglected the recognition aspect.

Another form of remuneration is a "fixed-formula" bonus where the workers are told exactly how much money they will earn if they achieve a certain level of productivity.

> A company approached me for help in designing a bonus scheme where various amounts of money would be linked to various levels of performance.
>
> I agreed to help them with the yardsticks for measuring the performance, but urged them not to throw their money away by converting potential rewards into remuneration.
>
> It is far more effective to focus on achieving good results and then to give a corresponding bonus to employees who have performed well.

Management can make use of a basic formula for determining the size of the bonus, but it should never become an official agreement that the employees can claim as their right.

Bonus or increase?

What form should the financial reward take? Many companies make use of differentiated salary or wage increases. In other words, good performers receive a greater salary or wage increase than the average performers. The problem with this approach is that it "perpetuates" the increase and leads to a great deal of distortion in the wage structure.

> Let's say that A is a star performer and B is average. Both are in the same job grade and both are earning R2 000 a month. At the end of the year A is given a R400 increase and B is given R200. This motivates A since it is a form of recognition for him, but let's say that B is determined to improve his work performance – and he does.
>
> We now have two star performers, so the following year both receive the top increase of R450. The next year they again receive a top increase of R500. What is happening month by month? Every month B is getting R200 less because three years ago he didn't perform so well.
>
> That doesn't seem right, so management decides to give B a R700 increase instead of R500, to bring him into line with A. This is only fair from management's point of view, but when A finds out, he is highly dissatisfied. Now we have even more problems.

Anybody who has ever worked with a company's salary structure will know how often the reward part of the increase is lost in an attempt to bring everybody into line with one another. They end up with salary adjustments rather than performance rewards.

A more effective system would be to give A the same increase as B and then to add a one-time amount (say, R2 400) in recognition of his achievements. In other words, employees should receive a large enough increase to maintain their standard of living as far as possible, but a bonus to reward them for excellent performance.

There are several advantages to this approach. One is that a bonus of

R2 400 has far greater impact than an additional R200 a month. It also allows for greater flexibility. The bonus for A could be R3 000 and for B R600. Finally, it means that A and B start off the new financial year on equal terms as far as their salaries are concerned.

Relative or absolute?

If money is to be used to motivate subordinates, the reward must be linked to performance, and management needs to understand that the relative amount has far greater impact than the absolute amount. For example, what would motivate A (the top performer) more: a bonus of R3 000 for himself and a bonus of R600 for B (the average performer), or a bonus of R5 000 for each of them? If A had to choose he would obviously choose R5 000, but the motivational impact of the R3 000 and R600 would be far greater, because it conveys the message that *management recognises the achievement*.

How much an employee gets by way of a merit bonus is not nearly as important as how much he gets *in comparison* with someone he regards as his peer. For that reason it is essential to make all merit rewards known, albeit in private. Management has to tell A that he (and maybe a few others) received the highest bonus because of his outstanding performance. Otherwise A may be under the impression that everybody was given that bonus – and the motivational impact is lost.

At the same time B should be told that he did not receive the highest bonus – that some people (without mentioning names) received as much as R3 000. He also needs to be told what he should do in order to qualify for the top bonus next year.

Such an approach is possible only if accurate records have been kept of each person's individual performance – and that takes us right back to the start of the management process, goal setting that will make the measurement of performance possible. It is an integrated approach.

Individuals or groups?

A number of management authors have advocated the use of group rewards. They argue that an individual seldom has control over the end result; it is the culmination of a team effort. I think that is a valid argument, and rewarding the group as a whole would not only be fair, but contribute to greater cooperation among the individual team members.

On the other hand, it can be argued that if an individual is doing an outstanding job while his colleagues are not doing much more than what is expected of them, it would be unfair to reward everyone on the performance of the group as a whole. The good performers are then very likely to lower their performance or look for a job where their efforts will be recognised.

Perhaps the best guideline is that, if an individual employee's performance can be clearly distinguished, and he is in a position where he is not heavily dependent on the input of others, he should be rewarded individually. If, however, it is difficult to distinguish individual contributions, the whole group should be rewarded and the team members given their share in proportion to their salaries.

Public or private?

In an earlier section I have stressed the importance of making the merit rewards known, without mentioning names. There have been companies where public presentations have not had any negative effect, but there have also been cases where public awards have led to social discrimination against the recipient.

> A security company near East London used to reward their security guards if they had prevented a crime or arrested somebody, by presenting them with a medal at a public parade the following morning. They could not understand, however, why so many of the recipients resigned shortly afterwards.
> When they stopped making the awards in public and presented the medals privately instead, the resignations also stopped.

There can be no hard and fast rule, but management needs to be sensitive to the possible effects that public awards can have on the recipient's relationship with his colleagues.

What about a performance appraisal system?

There are some very elaborate performance appraisal systems practised today, but most of them do more harm than good. It's not surprising that so many managers regard performance appraisal as one of the less pleasant aspects of their work, mainly because it forces them to sit in judgment on other people, especially if the system focuses on the character traits of the subordinate.

What is the purpose of a performance appraisal system? Some may claim that it is to give the subordinate feedback on his performance. If, however, an adequate control system is implemented, as suggested in chapter 15, the individual concerned will receive adequate feedback on an ongoing basis, and a formal appraisal system will be unnecessary.

Others may claim that performance appraisal is necessary to determine the extent of the financial reward that should be given to each employee. This is not a valid argument, since any manager worth his salt will know how well his individual subordinates have performed without having to sit down with them to complete a performance appraisal report.

Some people point out the value of having every employee's performance record on file in the personnel department with a view to promotion, transfers, and so on. There may be some merit in that, but the only information that needs to go on record is whether the individual's work performance is of such a nature that it requires special attention or not.

> The Ford Company in the United States has introduced a new approach to performance appraisal where employees are assessed and placed in one of three performance categories.
>
> The approach is based on the assumption that 80 per cent of employees are within the system, that is, they do their jobs as well as the system allows them to. About 10 per cent of employees are poor enough to be "outside the system" and therefore require attention, and another 10 per cent are excellent enough also to be "outside the system", requiring some action in the form of promotion, special recognition, or whatever (Scherkenbach 1985:40).

Probably the most important purpose of performance appraisal (perhaps the only purpose) is to help an individual subordinate map out some development programme for himself. This means that managers should sit down with their subordinates once a year to discuss their future career prospects and the experience and know-how the individual will need in order to equip himself for a higher position.

Obviously such a discussion does not have to be held with each subordinate since it is not applicable to all. Many secretaries, for example, may not aspire to higher positions, and to discuss career paths with them year after year would be rather meaningless.

The performance appraisal should be held about six months away from salary increase or bonus time, and not linked at all to financial rewards of any kind. When subordinates know that the outcome of the performance appraisal affects their pockets, there is a good chance that they will become very defensive. This will nullify any positive benefits that might have been gained from such a discussion.

Conclusion

Rewards play a very important role in motivating employees towards higher levels of performance, as long as they are used as a means of recognition for achievement. Managers who neglect the rewards available to them are neglecting some very powerful tools – to their own detriment.

Part 5
Conclusion

18 MANAGERS MAKE ALL THE DIFFERENCE

Scenario for the future

South Africa lies at the crossroads. We have a choice. In the words of Clem Sunter (1987:109) we can choose the low road or we can choose the high road. If we choose the low road, this beautiful country will become a wasteland in a very short space of time. Less than two decades ago Lebanon used to be the richest country in the Middle East. Today it is the poorest. It destroyed itself. There is a real danger that we will follow the same path unless we take some drastic steps to reverse the process.

If, however, we choose the high road, it will require an economic growth rate of at least 8 per cent per annum. While that is not impossible, it will depend to a large extent on the men and women who manage our business enterprises. They hold the key to raising the productivity of their subordinates.

Japan's exceptional economic achievement is mainly the result of their effective management approach – and those who have studied that approach have concluded that it has very little to do with their culture. There is no reason why South Africa cannot be just as successful economically. After all, we have more natural resources than Japan has.

The difference

All managers have a choice. They can either continue practising the traditional theory of management (or the human relations theory, which is just as ineffective), or they can start making a conscious effort to implement the human resource theory. It will make all the difference.

Let me conclude by summarising the differences between the traditional manager and the human resource manager:

The traditional manager	The human resource manager
Tells subordinates what they must do ☐ *Spells out activities step-by-step*	Tells subordinates what they must achieve ☐ *Leaves the initiative to them of how to achieve goal*
Sees subordinates as a help to himself ☐ *He is responsible for the work*	Sees himself as a help to subordinates ☐ *They are responsible for the work*
Takes most decisions for subordinates ☐ *He does the thinking – they switch off*	Allows subordinates to take most decisions themselves ☐ *They do the thinking – he reaps the benefits*
Does not tolerate mistakes from subordinates ☐ *Expects perfection but does not get it*	Uses mistakes as learning aid for subordinates ☐ *Encourages them to experiment with new ideas*
Says nothing about good performance but reprimands poor performance ☐ *Destroys subordinates' self-confidence*	Praises good performance and helps to correct poor performance ☐ *Motivates subordinates to achieve even more*
Controls work through inspection of activities ☐ *Conditions subordinates to look busy when he is around*	Controls work through measurement of results ☐ *Conditions subordinates to want to achieve*
Functions reactively ☐ *Reacts to what happens in the present*	Functions proactively ☐ *Makes things happen in the future*

The will to change

The management approach presented in this book is not new. Many managers are quite familiar with it because they have heard it so often – yet so few put it into practice. Why?

There are major barriers to bringing about change, and it is important for managers to recognise these, otherwise their good intentions will come to nought – like all the previous ones.

Firstly, it requires *the will to change*. It is estimated that about 10 per cent of managers really want to improve their managerial effectiveness, about 30 per cent are interested in doing so, 40 per cent aren't aware of the possibilities for changing, and about 20 per cent actively resist it.

Sadly enough it would seem that most of the 20 per cent that actively resist change are in top management positions. The reason for their resistance to change is understandable. The more successful one is, the smaller the need for change. Change can actually be very threatening, because it is an unknown area – and it may affect their positions of success. Yet for an organisation to develop a human resource management culture requires an active commitment (and practice) by top management.

The second barrier to change is closely linked to the first one, namely the *courage to change*. Change by itself implies an "admission" that past practices have not been as effective as they could have been. It takes a great deal of maturity and courage to admit that.

Thirdly, change requires *perseverance*. To change a management style is not easy and quite a few managers who have consciously changed their management approach have told me that the main problem does not lie with their subordinates, but with themselves. They had to work hard at changing their own way of thinking.

It must also be expected that subordinates will not always react immediately with enthusiasm. Often they are suspicious, or just scared of the new responsibilities that are confronting them. Initially they may make mistakes – and the temptation will be strong indeed to call the whole thing off.

> Several managers who have implemented the human resource approach have stressed the fact that many times they wanted to give up, but that they took a deliberate decision to persevere – until eventually they started reaping the benefits of a motivated work force.

Sometimes a change in management style also requires a change in the organisation structure, and in the decision-making authority granted to various employees. That can be very risky. It is unknown territory. Better the devil we know than the devil we don't.

It will take a good deal of willpower, courage and perseverance to implement the human resource management approach – but what is the alternative?

The choice

It all boils down to the fact that every manager has a choice. He can either break his subordinates down, or he can build them up. But he will eventually end up with the subordinates that he deserves.

APPENDIX

Performance areas and yardsticks

The yardsticks listed are examples of the type of measurement that can be used to evaluate an incumbent's job performance. It does not mean that the yardsticks given are the *only* ones that apply to that particular position – and it obviously depends on the exact nature of the job as to whether a particular yardstick will apply or not. These merely serve as illustrations of typical yardsticks that could be adapted for other positions as well.

Truck driver
- Fuel costs per kilometre
- Repair costs per kilometre
- Tyre life (kilometres)
- Average distance per hour (not to measure speed of travelling but time taken to effect deliveries)
- Number of times that the speed limit is exceeded (as per tachometer)

Dispatch supervisor
- Average load per truck
- Average time lapse between order and delivery
- Number of incorrect deliveries

Quality controller
- Number of rejects/complaints by customer/user
- Number of unnecessary rejects (as judged by boss)
- Number of avoidable problems not corrected

Mechanic
- Number of comebacks within one month
- Number of parts replaced unnecessarily
- Percentage time that was chargeable
- Value of tools replaced annually
- Number of mistakes on job/time card per month

Maintenance artisan
- Number of days behind/ahead of planned schedule
- Percentage deviation between planned and actual maintenance time
- Cost of maintenance/repairs (e.g. cost of spare parts)
- Number of "problem areas" not attended to

Construction foreman
- Days behind/ahead of schedule
- Days/hours of rework
- Rating for neatness
- Percentage material wasted
- Replacement cost of tools lost per annum
- Percentage deviation from budget

Admin/accounting clerk
- Number of mistakes per week
- Number of days over monthly/weekly deadline

Credit controller
- Amount of bad debts
- Number of "bad" customers
- Average time of decision to grant credit
- Percentage applications rejected
- Percentage of debt outstanding for 30, 60, 90 days and more
- Number/value of queries outstanding

Buyer
- Percentage overdue items
- Number of late purchases (number of orders not processed the same day)
- Percentage discount on published prices
- Number of incorrect purchases

Cashier
- Number of days not balancing the first time
- Amount over/under at end of each day
- Number of customer complaints (or corrections)

Secretary
- Number of typing mistakes per page
- Number of items referred to boss unnecessarily
- Number of "poor" messages taken
- Number of delays in file retrieval
- Number of client complaints

Telephonist (measured by sample surveys)
- Average number of times phone rings before being answered
- Number of times initial response is incoherent/curt
- Average time of waiting before going back to caller

Retail store manager
- Total sales volume
- Rate of stock turnover
- Average number of customers per day
- Percentage of dead stock
- Percentage losses on account of discounts
- Number of new accounts opened per month

Retail shop assistant
- Number of customers attended to (percentage of total customers)
- Average value of sale per customer
- Number of items returned by customer

Computer programmer
- Number of syntax errors per program
- Number of lines of code per day
- Percentage coverage (that is, how complete the program is)
- Number of "bugs" highlighted by user
- Number of queries from user (measuring quality of documentation)

Work study officer
- Boss's rating on quality of proposals (in terms of savings in money or time)
- Percentage changes by boss to final report
- Percentage implementation by user departments
- Days over/under deadline

Personnel officer
☐ Average time of settling grievances
☐ Average time of recruiting new staff
☐ Number of appointment recommendations rejected by line managers
☐ Amount of discussion time per month initiated with shop steward

Training officer
☐ Survey rating from trainees' managers on benefits of training programme
☐ Trainee-days (assuming that line managers have final say on how many of their subordinates attend training programmes)

Security officer
☐ Number of deviations from route schedule
☐ Number of cases where security information is insufficient
☐ Number of failed simulations
☐ Number of non-compliance situations (as per checklist)

Storeman
☐ Percentage deviation between actual stock and book stock
☐ Number of item-days out of stock
☐ Average value of stock on hand

There are three performance areas and yardsticks that apply to most management/supervisory positions:

Manpower management
☐ Personnel costs per output/turnover
☐ Percentage of proposed development plan accomplished
☐ Rate of absenteeism
☐ Rate of staff turnover

Loss control
☐ Man-hours lost on account of accidents
☐ Loss on account of shrinkage

Innovation
☐ Time spent on innovation or problem-solving discussions. (This means that a subordinate must report back on a weekly basis how much time he

spent with his subordinates on discussing the three key questions listed in chapter 13 – and what action plans have resulted from those discussions.)

"What you measure is what you get!"

Bibliography

Ball, A. & Asbury, S. (1989). *The winning way*. Johannesburg: Jonathan Ball.
Drucker, P. F. (1974). *Management: tasks, responsibilities and practices*. New York: Harper & Row.
Goddard, W. E. (1986). *Just-in-time: Surviving by breaking tradition*. Essex: Oliver Wright.
Goldsmith, W. & Clutterbuck, D. (1985). *The winning streak*. Middlesex: Penguin.
Hersey, P. & Blanchard, K. H. (1982). *Management of organisational behaviour: utilising human resources*. 4th ed. Englewood Cliffs: Prentice-Hall.
Herzberg, F. (1968a). "One more time: How do you motivate employees?" *Harvard Business Review* 46, 1.
Herzberg, F. (1968b). *Work and the nature of man*. London: Staples Press.
Humble, J. (1969). *Improving management performance*. London: Management Publications.
Hutchins, D. (1985). *Quality circles handbook*. London: Pitman.
Koopman, A. D., Nasser, M. E. & Nel, J. (1987). *The corporate crusaders*. Johannesburg: Lexicon.
Miles, R. E. (1975). *Theories of management*. Tokyo: McGraw-Hill Kogakusha.
Mol, A. (1981). *Let's both win*. Pretoria: Femina.
Mol, A. (1984). *Motivating your farm labourer*. Pretoria: Folio.
Mol, A. (1984). *Parenting isn't child's play*. Pretoria: Femina.
Peters, T. J. (1988). *Thriving on chaos*. London: Macmillan.
Peters, T. J. & Waterman, R. H. (1984). *In search of excellence*. New York: Harper & Row.
Scherkenbach, W. W. (1985). "Performance appraisal and quality: Ford's new philosophy". *Quality progress*, April 1985.
Sloan, A. P. (1972). *My years with General Motors*. New York: Doubleday.
Sunter, C. (1987). *The world and South Africa in the 1990s*. Cape Town: Human & Rousseau/Tafelberg.